GOT THE JOB...
NOW WHAT?

HOW TO MASTER THE CORPORATE GAME
FROM DAY 1

MORITZ DRESSEL

D1701929

WATLANKA PRESS
Got the Job... Now What?: How to Master the Corporate Game from Day 1
Moritz Dressel

Copyeditor: HappyMarli
Cover Design: Zeljka Kojic
Interior Design: JP Kusmin

Printed by CreateSpace, Charleston SC

ISBN 978-1540390202

Free Bonus Items

Free companion bonus items to this book, including checklists, email templates, printable versions of all graphics and tables, and more, are available at:

GotTheJobNowWhat.com/Bonus

Please access these resources now before you forget.

About the Author

Moritz Dressel is a management consultant specializing in post-merger integration, joint ventures, and strategic alliances. As a member of a leading M&A practice, he has supported major transformations in various industries, such as manufacturing, life sciences, and energy and utilities. He also is the author of the no. 1 handbook for consulting career starters, *The Aspiring Advisor*.

Dressel holds a BSc in Public Administration from the University of Twente, Netherlands, and an MSc in Management from the University of Lugano, Switzerland. He can be reached directly via Twitter @MoritzDressel or at moritzdressel.com.

Contents

Preface

When I started my career, I was lucky. Someone gave me an opportunity when I least expected it, but my good fortune didn't end there. In the following years, I had an opportunity to meet many other senior colleagues (at times, only senior by a few months) who were willing to share their wisdom. Although not all the advice seemed immediately useful to me, I ultimately realized that it made starting my career infinitely easier.

Nevertheless, there were a number of lessons that I learned the hard way that I would have rather done without. Over time, I have identified some approaches that work better than others, to prevent other people from going through the same struggles.

Being good corporate citizens, my colleagues and I passed on our wisdom to the new hires after us. Unfortunately, we couldn't simply hand over some guidebook with every relevant snippet of advice. Such a book didn't exist at that time.

Hence, in the summer of 2015, after a year of preparation, I published my first book, *The Aspiring Advisor*. It teaches readers how to start a successful career in the consulting industry. Based on my personal experience, as well as insights from both junior and senior colleagues alike, it contains the dos and don'ts that any consultant at the start of their career should be aware of.

After a little over a year since its release, it appears as though the market had indeed been waiting for such a publication. Many readers told me that they had taken away valuable lessons from the book even though they were not working in the consulting industry.

"Not everything is applicable in my job, but I am definitely going to try [BLANK]", was a recurring statement I heard from readers. Following that success, I decided to write yet another guide, but this time, it would be one designed for all those ambitious graduates who are seeking to start a corporate career, not necessarily just those in consulting.

I have personally worked on a number of international projects serving clients from various industries. Thus, I have had my fair share of insights beyond the consulting industry, but there is only so much one can learn from observation. Nothing is more insightful than actual practice, which is precisely why dozens of interviews with real people, who have already embarked on successful career journeys across a wide spectrum of industries, form the foundation of this book.

Despite certain differences between industries, there are common themes that came up in the interviews again and again (as expected). The result is this book—a practical compendium of what makes or breaks careers in larger organizations within the private sector.

WHO SHOULD READ THIS BOOK?

Anyone starting his or her career right out of college should flip through these pages. If you are going to work for a large corporation, this book is definitely for you. I have written this book with aspiring young professionals in mind. What would I have liked to know? What were the questions I asked my senior colleagues? Which questions were repeatedly raised by other new hires? *Got the Job... Now What?* has the answers.

WHAT IS COVERED?

The book begins at the point in the process where a graduate has signed a work contract. From well before the first day of work up to a potential resignation, common pitfalls and practical remedies are discussed in detail. While careers may differ, the intention is to equip any newcomer with the right tools to survive the first two to three years and lay the foundation for long-term career success.

Who Is This Guy?

I am currently working as an independent management consultant, and I previously worked at one of the leading global consulting practices. After about four years with the firm, I chose to take some time off to travel and learn new skills and languages. During that time, I decided to finally write the book that I would have personally liked to read when I started my career; so, somewhat by chance, I also became an author.

I hope that with *Got the Job... Now What?* career starters in other industries will be able to benefit, just like many consultants have already benefited from my previous book, *The Aspiring Advisor*. For some, it will be reassuring, and for others it might be eye-opening. Whatever purpose it serves for you, I wish you the best and would love to hear your story.

Berlin, Germany, November 2016

How to Use This Book

This book is structured along an aspiring young professional's "life cycle." Each of the four main parts is composed of different chapters focusing on a specific stage at the start of a recent graduate's career:

Part 1, "Groundwork," focuses on job entry preparation. It sets realistic expectations and details how to have a positive impact from the moment you start working.

Part 2, "Strategies and Tools," is all about getting things done. It provides useful tools, teaches vital skills, introduces key people, and lays out strategies to work the system in your favor.

Part 3, "Not In Your HR Brochure," is a more personal take on a variety of topics. It explains how to manage your private life, protect yourself from getting screwed by others, push back effectively, and find your sweet spot within the organization.

Part 4, "Fresh Start," acknowledges the fact that lifelong employment is dead. Multiple career tracks have become the new norm. As such, this part provides a career change decision-making framework as well as specific action steps to take when you are about to leave.

Getting the most out of this book is somewhat dependent on your background. There is a major difference between starting out right after college and already having a year of work experience. Hence, I suggest that you proceed as follows.

If You Are Just Starting Out

If you have just secured your first job at or have an interest in working for a large corporation, I would recommend that you read this book cover to cover at least once. In doing so, you will gain an in-depth understanding of how all the chapters come together and what it takes to succeed when just starting out. You can then go back to specific sections that have triggered your interest or that appear particularly relevant for your situation.

If You Already Have Some Experience

If you already have a few months (or years) of experience working in a large corporation, you're probably seeking some additional insights that you simply may have missed. Given that, reading this book cover to cover might not be the most efficient approach. Instead, I suggest that you quickly skim through the book to get an overall understanding of the content by reading each chapter's key takeaways and then proceed by reviewing specific sections of interest to you.

Example Case

Throughout this book, I will make reference to a fictional scenario that makes the concepts more tangible. I will illustrate certain concepts using realistic names and roles, rather than blank templates.

In the example, two companies have joined forces to speed up the development of a new technology. One of them is Future Technologies Inc. (FT), an innovative player in the growing augmented reality market based in Boston, MA. Their latest invention, the "TotalView", is a pair of smart glasses for industrial use. Remember Google Glass? Imagine that device on steroids.

Multiple companies have already voiced their interest in adopting this new device in their day-to-day operations, as they expect it to create significant efficiency gains. However, the "TotalView" is not ready to launch yet. Therefore, FT has teamed up with a leading logistics company, Global Trade Logistics Inc. (GTL), to test the product in real life. Currently, they are running a pilot in GTL's warehouse in Birmingham, UK, as part of their joint "Project Insight".

As part of the scenario, we will encounter the following stakeholders:

FUTURE TECHNOLOGIES INC. (FT)

- Mark Johnson (Junior-Level Resource): Mark is our main protagonist. He joined the company's finance department one year ago. You should relate to him; i.e., when you read "Mark," you may replace it with your own name.

- Jeremiah Smith (Chief Financial Officer): Jeremiah, the CFO of Future Technologies, is Mark's boss.

- Peter Jackson (Chief Executive Officer): Peter is the CEO of Future Technologies. Although FT is the market leader in augmented reality, he believes that "TotalView" can be a total game changer. Because of that, "Project Insight" with GTL is very high on his agenda.

- Manuela Perez (Project Lead): Manuela has been put in charge of managing "Project Insight". Unfortunately for her, there are no additional resources that are exclusively assigned to her. To accommodate that, Peter Jackson (CEO) and Jeremiah Smith (CFO) have agreed to have Mark support Manuela, if necessary.

GLOBAL TRADE LOGISTICS INC. (GTL)

- Bernard Cho (CEO): Bernard has been with GTL throughout his career and was recently appointed global CEO. One of his first objectives is to enhance the company's profitability. He believes that using technology to enhance daily operations is indispensable in that effort. To that end, he has started a number of initiatives, of which "Project Insight" is just one.

- Jacques Cazeneuve (Head of Europe): Jacques is in charge of the European market for GTL. Bernard has asked Jacques to make Europe more profitable and wants him to deliver results quickly. Jacques is also the Project Sponsor of "Project Insight".

- Robert Grant (UK Operations): Robert has been with GTL for more than twenty years and is the head of UK operations. He has been officially put in charge of "Project Insight" by Jacques. As such, he works closely with Manuela Perez of Future Technologies.

- Michael Gray (Head of Birmingham Warehouse): Michael is a GTL veteran at the Birmingham site. While he is close to retirement, he is excited about the opportunities that "TotalView" provides for their local operations.

- Andrew Seagull (UK Operations Analyst): Andrew is the "data guy" in GTL's UK operations team. He is heavily involved in "Project Insight" and will occasionally work with Mark Johnson.

You do not have to memorize this information. I will provide everything you need to know when referencing this project example. However, you might want to bookmark this page for easy reference.

Acknowledgements

Many people have played a role in making this book happen. In fact, there are too many to name them all.

First and foremost, I want to thank all of those who have shared their own perspective on career matters. The people that I interviewed during the research phase enabled me to write this guide for aspiring young professionals. Among those, I would like to give special thanks to Melissa Anchisi, Fabio Betti, Alexander Greinacher, Stefan Halters, Johan Jongejan, Taeyoung Kim, Roberto la Rocca, Jane Lam, Giulia Lanotte, Melania Mastinu, Valerio Pianezza, Alimur Rashid, Sara Ruggeri, Marco Siegenthaler, Sandra Theumann, Maria Vittoria Tomaini, Angelo Vassiliades, Priyesh Vyas, Antje Weiruss, Aerim Yoon, Örs Zekany, and Rebecca Zhang. Thank you!

I must also express my gratitude to those who have provided feedback on my previous book, *The Aspiring Advisor*, since it was published. Here, Martin Ruth and Constantin Ulmer stand out in particular. Your ideas have helped make this book more relevant. Thanks!

Special thanks go out to Giordano Siton for keeping me on track and Benjamin Schumann for helping me embark on this new book project. It's comforting to know that I have friends like you.

Finally, I have to thank all the readers of my previous book who do not work in the consulting industry. Without your feedback and encouragement, I probably would have never set out to write the book in front of you.

PART 1

Groundwork

PART 1 ESTABLISHES THE baseline for the rest of this book. As such, it focuses on the preparation for your job entry. Chapter 1 helps to set the right expectations. What is the world of business really like? Who will you be working with? What can you really contribute when you start? We will answer these questions (and many more) and destroy some of the most popular myths. Chapter 2 is all about Day 1 readiness. It lays the foundation for having a positive impact from the very first moment you enter the company.

[1]

What You Can Expect

"Reality is frequently inaccurate."

Douglas Adams,
The Restaurant at the End of the Universe

PEOPLE HAVE SHARED PLENTY of stories and anecdotes about the world of work. There are even books about (the dark sides of) specific industries. However, much of that is exaggerated and nowhere close to what you and I would experience on a day-to-day basis. Based on dozens of interviews and my own experience as a consultant working directly with numerous clients, this chapter will set a few things straight and help you start from a more realistic perspective. At the very least, it will save you from joining the corporate circus with complete naiveté.

First, I will share with you what you can expect in terms of your own role as a junior-level resource. I will then address a few popular misconceptions about the modern world of work, which often surprise newcomers. Our focus areas here will be industry reality, the variety of corporate workers, the role of "perfection", and the interaction between different hierarchical levels. Some of it will be surprising, if not amusing. Some of it also may be disappointing. However, rest assured, we will conclude this chapter on a positive note because, while not all that glitters is gold, you should be looking forward to joining the professional workforce.

YOUR ROLE

Breathe and get ready for some hard truths: When you're starting out, you are essentially an unproven asset. Even if you have been hired based on a referral, you have to prove your worth to the team. It doesn't matter what you've done before. Few people care about the university from which you graduated (actually, no one cares, unless they graduated from the same school). Your dissertation will have little to no value. Personal contacts that you may have outside the organization are also irrelevant to your professional career for the upcoming years.

This might sound overly harsh, if not outrageously subjective, so let us put this in proper context to really drive the point home. Consider Figure 1.

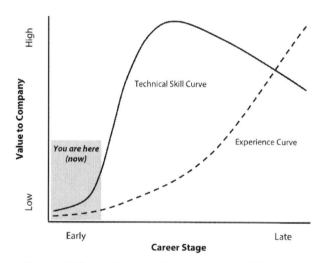

Figure 1: Value to Company Over the Course of the Career

From the perspective of a company, an employee has a certain value. If not, there is no point in keeping him or her on the payroll. Broadly speaking, what anyone can contribute is a combination of specific skills and experience. The type and content of both can vary greatly. However, if you look at it from a career progression perspective, there are a number of characteristics that apply, regardless of what industry and role are being discussed.

Skills and experience may be irrelevant if they don't properly fit in the organizational context. As such, both have value to companies—sometimes more, sometimes less. With respect to skills, it is commonly understood that career starters need to have proper training. Accept the fact that it will probably take you longer to get up to speed than you anticipate. Despite previous education, learning on the job is just as important in most industries as the continuation of formal training. For that reason, most companies invest heavily in their young employees. Soon, those new hires may develop into true assets to the company, as the value of the skills they obtain can increase fairly quickly.

However, such an increase may not continue indefinitely. Unless someone engages in constantly updating his or her expertise, a person's potential value for a company may diminish at a certain point. As I describe in Chapter 10, continuous learning is key. There are many professions where knowledge obtained five years ago is virtually useless today—a fact that you can observe in the declining skills value curve.

Experience, on the other hand, is a whole different ballgame. Junior-level resources usually don't have much, if any, professional experience. Gaining it cannot be forced. It simply takes time. While one can encourage exposure to different environments that provide learning opportunities, there is only so much that both an individual and a company can do to speed up that process. A certain degree of patience is essential. As you can see in the graph, experience can increase indefinitely, but its specific value to the company may vary. However, the fact that experience grows with increasing tenure is a matter of fact.

In a nutshell, career starters add limited expertise and negligible professional experience to their respective employer. Few people are true assets from Day 1. The true value lies in their potential for future development. No matter how you look at it, if you are just starting out, you are at the bottom of the food chain. This may affect your ego. It certainly affected mine. However, on the bright side, being in a junior role puts you in the invaluable position to be allowed to make (some) mistakes and learn from them.

So what does all of this mean for you in practice? Quite frankly, your key challenges are to get up to speed and build your personal brand. However, this is easier said than done. You will need to find people who trust in you and who will provide you with opportunities to learn. Over time, you will be able to develop a solid technical skill set (i.e., expertise) that can then serve as a platform to become "known" for something.

Many new hires get this sequence wrong. Typically, having graduated from leading schools and often having been best in their respective classes, the expectation is to excel from Day 1. The truth is, this is rarely the case. Even so, given some degree of ignorance, many believe that they have the right to stand for something unique and original from early on. My advice: Don't. It *will* backfire.

According to Seth Godin, "You earn the right to be heard. If there's a sick person on the plane, the doctor in 3b has the right to speak up; the hysterical person behind her does not."[1] Likewise, you will also have to pay your dues first. You have to earn your "right" to become a brand within the company. That being said, it does not have to take long. A few stellar performances go a long way. Think extra mile, not Ironman.

Long story short, in everything you do, be humble, work hard, and seek to improve every day. While doing that, keep building meaningful relationships by proactively introducing yourself and supporting those you know. Don't consider any task too mundane or boring. People do recognize when junior members go the extra mile. Organize drinks? Go for it. Get the documents bound yourself? Why not? Everybody knows that it's not ideal, but someone has to do it. With the right attitude, it will get easier and pay off in the future.

Your Colleagues

With respect to your colleagues, it probably comes as no surprise that there is no "standard" corporate employee. People differ. Some industries might attract a certain type of character more than others, but at the end of the day, you will find that any organization is largely a reflection of society. You will meet people from all walks of life. The differences can be insignificant or they may matter greatly. Here are some aspects where your colleagues may differ that you should be aware of.

- **Education:** Unless you are starting to work in an industry that requires a specific type of degree (e.g., lawyers, doctors), educational backgrounds will likely differ among your colleagues. Even within specific subsets of corporations, you will often find great variance in terms of professional qualifications. Not everyone in the HR department will have studied human resources. Likewise, the supply chain team does not necessarily consist of people trained in logistical operations. Regardless of the department, don't be surprised to see a broad mix of educational backgrounds. This is because, on the one hand, degrees appear to be a poor indicator of true qualification.[2] On the other hand, this day and age requires teams to have a broad spectrum of perspectives. This can hardly be achieved when everyone is equipped with the same degree. In fact, research shows that "diversity across dimensions, such as [...] education [...] can increase performance by enhancing creativity or group problem-solving."[3] Fresh and novel perspectives require different viewing angles of the starting point.

- **Profession:** When you are just starting out, the people on your level most likely have a similar professional background to yourself. The company is probably their first real work experience, just as it is for you. However, when it comes to more senior colleagues, you will realize that there are people with all types of professional backgrounds. Some senior figures might have started out just like you and worked their way up the corporate ladder, but this species is dying out.[4] There will be plenty of others who have only joined the company at a later stage in their careers. These include both those joining from competitors and those joining from entirely different industries. Do not expect to meet only industry veterans.

- **Motivation:** People have different priorities based on their background and experience. You will meet some colleagues who give their utmost at all times. Working towards the corporate mission is what gets them up in the morning. However, they are the exception. You will find just as many who regard their role merely as any other job, perhaps one that will land them a position elsewhere years down the road. Also, some may be perfectly happy about business-as-usual, while others really want to make a difference. Thus, do not expect everyone to share the same level of enthusiasm as you. Keep in mind that those who matter within corporations usually have a great deal of ambition and drive. It is those people who you should side with on a day-to-day basis if you want to succeed in the long run.

- **Generation:** In terms of age differences, you should not underestimate the potential impact of generational gaps within work environments. While it may be amusing to see some senior folks struggle with technological change, it likely does not matter on a daily basis. It certainly should not matter to you. Instead, all your effort should be spent in making sure the possible generational gap is not inhibiting your own development. Be aware of the fact that younger generations (e.g., Gen Y) may sometimes be perceived as rather overconfident, not open to feedback, potentially lazy, more interested in the *life* part of their work-life balance than in actual work, and open to the idea that there may be different ways to accomplish things.

You could write an entire book about the aspects that differentiate people in larger organizations. For now, this is meant to provide a taste of the different characteristics of the people you will meet and work with. Just remember, people simply come from all walks of life.

EXPECTATION VS. REALITY

Whatever people promised you that your tasks would be in your new role, the reality of your role will often hit hard. Expectations are rarely accurate. Whatever you may expect to experience in your new company, chances are that the truth of it will be different. If your expectations are based on popular media, this hard truth is particularly relevant. What you see presented in TV series (e.g., Mad Men, House of Lies) is not what the average person in the industry actually experiences. Obviously, this is because everything *entertaining* needs a little bit of drama. The actual work in the industry is far more mundane than producers would like us to believe. In fact, there are typically a lot more spreadsheets than glamour. Reality is also much slower, routine-based, and down to earth than what you may expect. In short, no actual industry matches its depiction in the media. Therefore, get in touch with those who have first-hand experience either by reaching out personally or reading relevant industry accounts.

One last thing.... No matter how hip and trendy many corporations try to appear, do not buy into it until you have confirmed it for yourself. There are countless initiatives in many organizations with the goal of modernizing the way things are done. Encouraging entrepreneurship, becoming more agile, abandoning personnel evaluation...the list goes on and on. Some of these initiatives succeed, and some don't. Some others get a big rush of media attention, but for whatever reason (e.g., too much work, organizational resistance to change) the initiatives are never implemented. Make no mistake: corporations are organizations made up of people. No matter how fancy a concept may sound, and no matter how supportive the board may be, the reality of having to get stuff done on a daily basis is often a challenge.

There is a plethora of surprises you will likely experience in your job, but there is only one effective way to deal with it: get used to it. Do not boil the ocean. Just because you expected something different does not justify you complaining from the very beginning. Suck it up, give it your best, and see how it goes. If after a month or two the situation has not changed, speak with your manager (or mentor). Sometimes you simply have to grow into a new role.

THE MYTH OF PERFECTION

The revelation that corporate life is often different from what many expect is no longer news. One such area often concerns the sophistication—if not the demand for perfection—within most corporations. However large or famous an organization may be, chances are good that there is significant room for improvement.

If you've never worked in the corporate world before, you will be surprised to see what the working reality is actually like. Sometimes, you begin to wonder how some companies can successfully operate, let alone generate a profit. This applies to small companies and Fortune 500 companies alike. Examples are manifold and often include:

- **Technology:** Given the complexity of most large organizations, you would expect corporate leaders to have an interest in adopting the latest technologies. After all, what enables us privately in ways previously unimagined should also be useful in business. However, the reality is different. Legacy systems often stand in the way of significant improvements. Also, for most companies, risk management is of the utmost importance. Therefore, you should quickly come to accept that your privately used devices are probably miles ahead of what you will be using in your job. In other words, you may have a Ferrari at home but a horse carriage at the office. There is no need to complain about these specific challenges to your peers. Everyone knows. Depending on your company, the exact shortcomings may differ, but rest assured, you may be disappointed if you expect perfection in terms of:

  - Intuitive and fully functioning enterprise resource planning systems (fun fact: not all companies can actually tell how many people they employ, nor who they are)

  - A powerful knowledge-sharing platform (that is also fairly up-to-date and used frequently)

- Integrated learning platforms (e.g., training calendar per grade, results automatically captured in a performance management system, etc.)

- Accurate customer/client relationship management tools

- State-of-the-art collaboration and task management tools

- **Internal Processes:** Processes are not always as clear-cut and straightforward as one would expect. Don't be surprised if you experience, for example, lengthy, nontransparent decision-making processes or realize that you don't have access rights to the financial reporting system requiring you to authorize certain payments due to being assigned to a different legal entity in the IT system... you get the picture. Redundant work and extra loops in internal processes are common in even the most famous corporations.

INTERACTION BETWEEN LEVELS

Now, let's consider the interaction between different hierarchical levels. Whatever people try to make you believe, expect the worst when it comes to how "easy going" a work environment really is. If you find yourself in a flat hierarchy, good for you, but do not be surprised if you experience the opposite. The hierarchical mindset—the perceived relationship between senior- and junior-level employees—with which some of your colleagues will enter the professional world can still be rather startling.

The most common issue is related to the delegation of work. For example, at some point, you will end up working for people who will delegate either a) everything or b) only those tasks that would be commonly called "shitty jobs." Fortunately, you will learn something from every task you undertake at the start of your career.

This becomes more problematic once you have performed certain tasks many times over and you realize that the only reason you are being asked to do it again is because your senior colleague is a) too lazy or b) does not have a clue how to do it him- or herself. These moments are painful, and we have all gone through them (for specific guidance on how to turn down work requests, refer to Chapter 17).

Similarly, some individuals, regardless of their level, are happy to forget the team spirit when it comes to their own private matters. Don't get me wrong; there should be a life outside work. But leaving with a hypocritical, *"But don't stay too long,"* while expecting juniors to work until the wee hours of the morning is just wrong.

Both of these examples are just that—examples. There are many other situations in which you can experience the hierarchical food chain in practice. The problem is, many juniors get so fed up that by the time they are in a senior position, they consider it perfectly normal to engage in the same behavior. Don't let that happen to you. Be better. Apart from those "senior exploits junior" anecdotes, you will likely be in awe once you see your (potentially) hellish manager cowering in front of his boss. Some people become so fixated on their next promotion that it becomes hard for them to speak up. Even if they have a point, you will rarely see your seniors correct their boss. It does happen but not often enough.

ON THE BRIGHT SIDE

Despite what I've touched upon so far, you should look forward to starting your new job. I am of the firm opinion that you can learn something from every first work experience. This is also what all of those people interviewed for this book expressed. No matter how suboptimal the situation may have been at the beginning, everyone was able to learn valuable lessons and ultimately viewed the issue as a crucial stepping-stone in their career.

You will meet people with different backgrounds and different mindsets. There will also be people you will quickly learn to avoid. However, there will be plenty of others who will happily have you on their team and will support you in your development. Suck it up when you interact with the former, and start seeking out the latter (yes, changing teams within organizations is possible).

Clearly, it will not always be easy, and you may have to go the extra mile—which is not just a catchy phrase, by the way, but means that you actually have to do more than is being asked or even paid for. Have ambition as well as patience. Trust that the hard work will pay off eventually, but maybe not after just a week or even a month. You will run into obstacles, but you will also learn from them. You will meet resistance and unfair treatment, but you are more than capable of growing through it. The effort you put in will be noticed. Just make sure the output is top quality too, and you will be set for a solid career start.

KEY TAKEAWAYS

- Know yourself first. In your new job, you should fully understand your own role before anything else. Only then can you appropriately navigate the work environment and appeal to your (senior) colleagues.

- Roll up your sleeves. You have to become a valuable asset quickly. Help keep the company running, and do not limit yourself to what is included in your job description.

- Be open to working in a diverse organization. Your colleagues come from all walks of life, and you might not have anything in common besides handing out the same business card.

♦ Prepare for spreadsheets, not glamour. Whatever you may think the world of work is like, even if your opinions are based on popular media, it is likely going to be different.

♦ Don't set your hopes too high, as most corporations are not the epitome of perfection. Whether related to technology or internal processes, expect to find plenty of room for improvement.

♦ Stay close to true leaders. Don't get bogged down by hierarchical games. Instead, identify and connect with those who lead, not solely by virtue of rank but by example.

♦ Expect setbacks, but be confident in the knowledge that you can have a very rewarding career start if you continue to seek out learning opportunities and develop yourself.

[2]

Getting Ready for Day 1

> *"Readiness is all."*
>
> **William Shakespeare, *Hamlet***

FIRST IMPRESSIONS MATTER. AT a time where first-impression apps like Tinder flourish, few would argue that appearance is unimportant at first sight. This chapter attempts to set you on the right track by illustrating how to lay the groundwork for a successful career.

To a large degree, it is when people meet for the first time that opinions about one another are made. In fact, the initial meeting is often the very beginning of the relationship that determines its future. Whether you will "click" with your colleagues is largely dependent on how they perceive you upon first being introduced to you. This is what we will delve into in this chapter.

First, I will emphasize the importance of Day 1 readiness and why so many people fail at it. We will then look more closely at what Day 1 readiness means for you and how to achieve it.

WHY DAY 1 READINESS?

Day 1 readiness is a classic business term that is commonly used in large-scale transformation projects. Day 1 readiness defines the minimum criteria to be met in order to pass a key milestone in a project plan. What every project team is working toward is the day when a new "reality" sets in (e.g., a new IT system goes live or a legal separation is completed).

Why does this matter to you? In a way, you need to prepare yourself for your own Day 1. It is your first day on the new job and most likely your first day at work ever. You are joining the real world now. To facilitate a smooth transition, you will want to set yourself up for success. Thorough preparation serves this purpose.[5]

WHAT MOST PEOPLE GET WRONG

Most career starters should get much more out of their first work experience. What got them into the job is actually quite close to what will also get them ahead. When applying, most people invest an enormous amount of time preparing for job interviews, assessment centers, brainteasers, etc. Landing the job usually takes time, but practice does eventually make perfect.

However, once the contract has been signed, many people go back on autopilot. Celebrating your entry into your dream industry is great, but starting without special preparation is not. Don't get me wrong, celebrations and quality time have their place, but I believe that everyone should at least squeeze in an hour or two thinking through what needs to happen for a successful first day at work. I hope that the previous two sections drove home the importance of systematically preparing for your own Day 1.

OBJECTIVES FOR YOUR DAY 1

Put yourself in the shoes of your future colleagues for a moment. What kind of person would you like to have on your team or project? Which character traits would you value most? Also, what would turn you off or earn the new hire a spot on your mental blacklist (i.e., you would not consider him or her for a spot on your team)? If you were to ask my colleagues, some of those interviewed, and me, we would tell you something like the following:

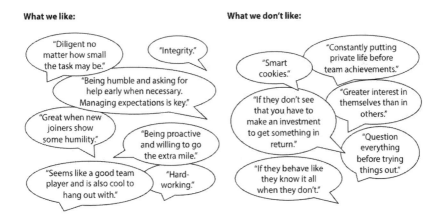

Objective	You want to come across as being...
Likeability	Humble, modest, sociable, essentially a "nice guy," conveying an interest in other people
Drive	A self-starter, looking for ways to accomplish things, helpful to the team, proactively asking how to support best
Motivation	Interested in the work of other people, willing to work hard, conveying a sense of pride to be part of the company
Client readiness *(if applicable)*	Reliable, trustworthy, professional, sharp, knowing your own role (junior vs. senior, product/service provider vs. client)

Table 1: Day 1 Objectives

From this, we can derive a specific set of objectives that you should take to heart (Table 1). Remember that people are often short on time, so they have to form an opinion quickly. Therefore, the closer you can be to meeting these objectives by coming across accordingly, the brighter your future in the company is likely to be.

WHAT TO PREPARE FOR DAY 1 AND HOW

There are a million ways that someone starting out in a new job can prepare. Most of that preparation is industry-agnostic, meaning that some of the information is applicable, regardless what industry you join. Generally speaking, you want to prepare yourself to successfully meet the previously discussed Day 1 objectives.

To accomplish this, focus on both yourself and everything external that is of relevance. This is easier than you may think. Yet, if the interviews conducted for this book are any indication, some junior-level resources still appear to fail at this task miserably time and time again.

PERSONAL ASPECTS TO CONSIDER

First of all, you want to ensure you come across as a valuable asset to the team. Pretending won't be enough. You will have to deliver quality work, which will ultimately be the relevant measure of success. However, when you are starting out—really on your first day—this should not be your major concern. You want to focus on making a positive first impression, as it will likely be a lasting one. More specifically, you should consider your appearance, your professional and personal online profiles, and your personal pitch.

YOUR APPEARANCE

Approach your first day (or week) at work as if you were going on a date. According to relationship expert Leil Lowndes, "The way you look and the way you move is more than 80 percent of someone's first impression of you."[6] You want to look great but not overdo it. Obviously, there are different dress codes in different industries. In fact, at times, they even vary between offices within the same company. Adopting the industry style is great, but you can blend in later. Show up in whatever you wore during the interview process. This will usually keep you on the safe side.

If you are still unsure, ask yourself: *What did the people who interviewed me wear? What do employees featured on their website or in their brochures look like?* If none of this helps, reach out to the recruiting team of your new employer.

Obviously, you don't want to go into debt just to look good on Day 1. Investing in quality items will come at a price. What follows below are the essentials, which should set you back less than a month's salary. If that still means you need to borrow money, then by all means go ahead and do so, but don't come to work looking like a car crash. You have to look smart, if only to make a first good impression.

The following are things you should consider:

- **Clothing:** For most professional work environments, appropriate clothing includes suits, shirts, and ties for men, pant or skirt suits and blouses for women, and appropriate shoes. Nothing else is required for now, or at least it is not critical for Day 1. Keep things simple. Don't try to impress people just yet. Be practical. Think *House of Cards* rather than *Great Gatsby*. Fashion statements can wait.

  When establishing your new wardrobe, focus on items that can be easily matched with one another. You should avoid items that can only be worn in combination with one other item. Avoid limiting yourself. Buy at least two or three suits. This goes for both men and women. Navy blue suits work very well for most. Stay away from black suits unless you want to leave the impression that you're coming from a funeral. I personally prefer to have different colors to add some variety. You should also own a substantial amount of business shirts or blouses. For starters, make sure to have at least ten business shirts or blouses of good quality. The more you have, the lower the likelihood of running out of clean articles of clothing due to a busy workweek (or weekend). Focus on white and light-blue shirts or blouses for now. They are the most versatile and can be combined with pretty much anything.

- **Shoes:** Your shoes also do not need to make any statement other than showing that you are ready to do professional work (e.g., meeting clients, attending board meetings). Let me say that again: fashion statements are not required. It should come as no surprise that your shoes should be spotless. If necessary, give them a shine before you leave the house—especially on your first day. *Note:* If you already own decent shoes, make sure that the heels are in good condition. If they're not, fix them. Buy at least two pairs of good-quality shoes. They should match your suits. I recommend owning a pair of black and dark brown shoes. If you want to get a third pair, get another in black, as you will likely use these more often. Furthermore, each pair should match with whatever belts you plan on wearing (if applicable).

- **Hair:** Get a professional haircut a week before you start. You do not want to look as if you just came from the hairdresser, nor as though you have not seen one for a while. Try to look normal. If you're completely clueless as to what this means in your industry, go to the career pages of your company and check out what other junior-level resources look like. If you are male, your grooming does not stop here. You also need to shave. To all the hipsters out there: facial hair is frowned upon. Regardless of what fashion magazines may tell you, most industries are more conservative than you think. There is no need to sport a beard—at least not in the beginning. Remember, it is all about Day 1 readiness here. If you want to grow a beard, there will be opportunities to do so in the future.

- **Bag:** Buy a decent professional bag that you would be happy using on a daily basis. If you are supposed to carry around a work laptop regularly, then the small leather briefcase that you've seen in the movies is not the right choice. You won't even be able to use it until you become Vice President or higher. Consider anything that is durable, high quality, and can fit both a laptop (ideally, fifteen-inch screen size) and some documents. It does not hurt to go for big brands here, but don't overdo it. Bringing a brand-new designer bag on Day 1 would be inappropriate in most companies.

  In addition, think ahead and consider how you will travel with your new bag. Can you easily strap the bag on top of a carry-on trolley? If not, look elsewhere. Depending on your industry, you might receive a standard laptop bag, backpack, or trolley on your first day. They might be practical, but you would be an exception if you were to use those beyond your first week or two. Most people prefer using something they really like instead of what they just received for free. Furthermore, free bags have the tendency to fall apart quickly.

There are additional items you could consider giving a makeover or replacing. For now, focus on the above, noting that these constitute the bare minimum. Do not waste time and money on items (e.g., expensive pens, cuff links) that will not necessarily help you get ready for Day 1. You will have time to develop your own personal style over time, but that should not be your objective at the start.

In general, you should feel comfortable with your appearance. I understand that some people might not be used to wearing suits, but don't let this stop you. Instead, simply get used to it. If you have to, wear your outfit for weeks before your official start. Don't settle for excuses.

Clearly, the above guidelines assume that you work in a traditional professional work environment with potential customer (or client) interaction. If you happen to work in a more casual office environment, this will also be reflected in the dress code. Make sure to clarify that as part of your Day 1 preparation.

Your Professional Online Profile

Make sure you update your professional online profiles, such as those on LinkedIn or Xing, before you start to work. This will serve two purposes. First, your update might show up in your new colleagues' newsfeed. Nothing conveys motivation and commitment to the company better than an updated profile stating that you are now working for that company before Day 1.

Second, you will be adding new people to your network from the first day you start your new role. Do not put them off by stating something other than the fact that you are employed at that company. You might think that still claiming to be a student in your profile would not matter, but you're wrong. What does that say about your diligence? What does it say about how organized you are?

Will all this matter on a large scale? No, of course not, but we are not talking about the large scale. We are talking about the building blocks for Day 1 readiness. This is one of them.

YOUR PERSONAL ONLINE PROFILE

You will also want to carefully review your personal online profiles (e.g., Facebook, Twitter, Instagram). Spend some time deleting anything that others might deem inappropriate. This includes incriminating pictures, posts, and likes. Don't become a victim of your past. At the very minimum, ensure that your privacy settings are such that new colleagues and future clients cannot view information that could potentially damage your reputation.

YOUR PERSONAL PITCH

In the beginning, you will meet plenty of new faces on a daily basis. For the most part, you will only have brief chats. These will rarely consist of anything more than the usual welcome and perhaps a brief chat about your background, but do not come unprepared. Instead, think of an elevator pitch. Carefully read through the following questions, and think of succinct answers:

1. Who are you? Think: What is your name? Where are you from? What is this place known for? These will be the most frequently encountered topics in your early days. Make them succinct and to the point, but also make sure that they are somewhat memorable. No need to be a comedian, but try to stand out with something interesting.

2. What did you do before? Think: Where did you study, and what? What type of relevant job experience have you had before, if any? Be clear about your educational background. If you studied something that most of your

friends and relatives would not understand just by its title, think of a brief explanation to clarify your expertise.

3. Is this your first time working in this industry? Think:
    How can you prove that you have what it takes to become
    an asset to the company or team? Mention any prior ex-
    perience that is relevant (if any). If this is indeed your
    first time working in this industry, convey your will-
    ingness to learn and your commitment to roll up your
    sleeves and work hard.

4. Where will you be based? (If applicable) Think: Which
    office will you primarily be working from? If you had a
    choice, why did you choose that location? Do not get too
    personal here. Respond by stating the place and explain-
    ing that this made the most sense in order to be close to
    your team or potential clients.

5. Which team will you join? Think: Who is your team lead?
    Who will you be working with? What will you likely be
    working on? Do not assume that everyone is familiar
    with the corporate setup. Organizational charts and
    leadership roles change too frequently for everyone to
    remember or stay up to date. Therefore, provide some
    easy point of reference by mentioning your team lead,
    other key people, and key propositions.

6. Why did you want to join our company or the team?
    Think: Why did you choose this company, and what par-
    ticularly excites you about the team you joined? People
    will assume that joining their company was the only or
    one of the only options you had. Given that, do not get
    too carried away here. There's no need to say that this

company was the best in the market . . . Be realistic. Remember, they know the company better than you.

7. What do you hope to get out of your experience with our company? Think: Why did you choose to start a career in this industry? For now, assume you will stay around forever, even if you regard this only as an entry point into a promising career elsewhere.

External Aspects to Consider

Making sure that you will be perceived in the best light possible is only the first step. Your Day 1 preparation should also include a number of background checks about your new workplace. You should get a good sense of the organization you are going to join. For this you will have to dig deeper into who you will be working with (background of new colleagues), where this is going to take place (logistics), and in what context you will be working (portfolio and organizational design).

Background of New Colleagues

By the time you have accepted your offer, you will probably have had contact with multiple future colleagues from your company. Some will have met you during job interviews, while others might have contacted you by email or phone. In short, you should have at least a handful of names of future colleagues already available.

With those in hand, conduct some research on those people that you already know. This is not unethical but an essential ingredient to allow you to quickly click with your new coworkers. There are different ways to do this. Here is what I would recommend as the most practical:

1. Sign out from your professional network accounts (e.g., LinkedIn). You want to avoid your name popping up in

each of your new colleagues' updates about "people who have reviewed your profile."

2. Do a quick Google search of each of your new contacts and see what comes up.

3. Go to the most relevant professional networks and search for your new contacts.

4. Print or save their profiles, and read them a few times prior to Day 1.

The objective of this exercise is not to stalk but to get a better understanding of those with whom you will be working. In particular, professional profiles posted online are often a good indication of how people see themselves or how they would like to be seen.

LOGISTICS

You must not arrive late at the office on Day 1. Even if you will "only" be meeting people from HR, you can be certain that some type of feedback will be passed on to your manager. Therefore, make sure you know exactly where your new office is. Ideally, you should visit the location beforehand (use Google Street View at least). You don't want to be late on your first day simply because you couldn't find the entrance.... Also, ensure that you are clear about how to get to the building from your home and how long the trip will take.

PORTFOLIO AND ORGANIZATIONAL DESIGN

Finally, you will want to review the entire product or service portfolio of your new company, particularly as it pertains to your team. This is key. You will probably be slightly confused on Day 1, but prior preparation will help you settle in much more quickly.

Apart from your own team, try to get an overall understanding of how the organization is structured. What organizational units exist? What do they do? Who is in charge? What's the overall strategy?

What major industry trends are they facing? If you join a smaller organization, this will be a no-brainer. In larger organizations, it will probably take a while before you've fully grasped the complexity (if that is even possible).

You will probably be introduced to these topics on your first day, but do not wait for others to spoon-feed you when you can get this information yourself. Just as re-reading a book will often reveal new insights, this task will enable you to make better connections and, potentially, come up with better questions during the Q&A session.

All of this does not have to happen in isolation. If you can find intelligent ways to connect with your new boss (or other colleagues), then by all means do so. Proactively reaching out before starting the job is appreciated. For example, before joining, you could contact your boss via email asking to swing by for coffee. Chances are that you will end up being invited to some upcoming team meeting or something similar where you will be introduced even before your official starting day. This happens all the time, and you should take advantage of such opportunities.

Key Takeaways

- Make a good first impression. Ensure that you appear sharp on Day 1. Don't get lazy after signing the work contract. Seek excellence in your first encounter with your new company as an employee too. This requires effort.

- Serve Day 1 objectives. Consider doing anything that helps other people recognize you as likeable, driven, motivated, and, if applicable, client-ready.

- Prepare yourself. Focus on essentials first, namely your appearance, updated professional and personal online profiles, and a succinct introduction pitch.

♦ Deliver your message. When you are introduced to new colleagues, you will be asked the same questions again and again. Make sure you nail your responses the first time around using your script.

♦ Investigate beforehand. Do some research about your new company and colleagues. The more you learn in advance, the easier you can connect and cope with potential information overload at the start.

PART 2

Strategies and Tools

PART 2 IS ALL about getting things done without going crazy. Chapter 3 provides specific action steps to successfully survive your first week and lay the foundation for future excellence. Chapter 4 adds to this by outlining the different stakeholders that will be most relevant for you in the first week or two and details how to build fruitful relationships.

Chapters 5–10 focus on developing the specific skill set needed to actually become a resourceful employee and a true asset to your company. Finally, Chapters 11–14 conclude this part by illustrating how to work the system in your favor and advance your career within the realm of your current employer.

[3]

Surviving Your First Week

"The beginning is the most important part of the work."

Plato, *The Republic*

WHEN YOU START YOUR first week, you will go through a sequence of different phases. We will start by looking at what a typical kick-off session at your new company could look like. Subsequently, you will have your first real encounter with members of your team. We will review what this will be like and what can go wrong during that interaction.

Toward the end of your first week, you will have your initial practical experience on the job. Chances are your expectations will not be completely met. That's fine. We will address some of the topics that come up at this point and will specifically flesh out what you should do in your first week to establish yourself on a strong foundation in order to excel.

INDUCTION DAY(S)

Wherever you start, you will likely go through an introductory session with other new hires. At times, these sessions may last several days or even multiple weeks. Oftentimes, it is just a one-day affair. Let us briefly clarify what you are likely going to hear, who you are going to meet, and what to pay particular attention to.

THE PURPOSE AND CONTENT OF INDUCTION EVENTS

The purpose of induction events is to provide an overview of the corporation, including its history, organizational design, product or service portfolio, ways of working etc. Often, regulatory requirements will be fulfilled as well, such as informing new hires about certain industry rules, professional standards, or ethical behaviors and requesting a sign-off thereof.

PEOPLE YOU MEET DURING THE INDUCTION

Depending on your company's size and hiring strategy (i.e., how often people are recruited during a year), your first day at work will likely be unique. You may be sitting in a room of ten or in a hall of three hundred. Also, do not expect to exclusively meet fellow junior-level resources. Sometimes, there will be a mix of different levels (including seniors).

On the other hand, you will get to know the instructors, who are usually from the HR department, or other employees with specific expertise that will be shared during the induction session. Use these brief encounters to make a good impression. Be nice, smile, ask intelligent questions (if you have any, otherwise remain silent), and involve yourself in friendly chats during breaks.

FINAL REMARKS ON INDUCTION DAYS

You will be sitting in a room full of people with a great deal of ambition. This is a fantastic situation to be in. Unfortunately, some people use induction events as self-promotion platforms. Don't be one of those people.

Do not boast about your educational merits or other details you think may impress others.[7] You simply don't know what your relationship with those in attendance will be. Will you be working on the same team or related projects? Will one of the new hires be your senior? Is HR instructed to report back the new hires' performance to each team? Don't take any risks.

So, how should you behave? Imagine that you were invited to a friend's wedding. You are one of the guests, but you probably will not know many people besides the bride and the groom who invited you. Using common sense, what would you naturally do in such a situation? Be open, smile, and show interest in other people.[8]

If you do all of the above at the induction event, you will be off to a good start. The induction event is not the right platform to make lasting impressions. Settle first; excel later.

MEETING YOUR NEW TEAM

At some point, you will meet your new team. The team will probably be different from what you expect. Let me crush your dreams for a moment.... By and large, every team is happy to have additional resources. As such, they will welcome you as best they can. However, "best" is usually very close to "not good."

Your team members will likely welcome you with kind words, but they are also thinking about how they can get their own work done before the deadline. Here's the deal: no one says, "Hell, yeah!" when being asked to onboard new colleagues unless they have nothing else to do.

Accordingly, you will likely run through some generic checklists with a colleague on how to find your way through your new corporate world, including the intranet, knowledge exchange system (if any), time reporting, etc. For the benefit of both you and your colleague, do not waste each other's time by trying to understand all the details immediately. Be nice and cut it short. Your colleague will appreciate it.

That being said, what do you do if you really do not understand something? Quite simply, ask. However, ask other people. First, you should let your colleague off the hook and see if you can figure it out yourself (unless you are drawn onto some important work right away). If you cannot, then reach out to the people you met during the induction. They will probably have dealt with the same topics, and this is also a good way to connect again (*read:* networking).

Alternatively, you can use your gaps of understanding as a handy reason to reach out to people around you who you have not met yet. It gets a bit tactical here, but bear with me.... Introduce yourself, have a quick chat, and leave. After an hour or so, bring up whatever topic remains unclear, and see if your newest acquaintance has the capacity to help out or knows someone who can. There is more to tell about the people you will meet in your first few days. For more information, see Chapter 4.

Disillusionment

Chances are, there will be moments that make you doubt your decision to join your company. I have tried to put things into perspective in Chapter 1 and argued that even joining famous organizations is no guarantee for encountering excellence on all levels.

Now, let's look at the most common challenges that juniors experience in their first days and discuss what you can do to navigate your way through them.

People Are Not Available

Depending on your type of work, you might realize that you cannot meet your whole team immediately when you are just starting out. It may take some time for you to meet key team members in person.

This can be particularly frustrating if those with whom one has had contact before (e.g., during job interviews) are not available. There is very little you can do about this. Face the situation as-is and make the most of it. Sooner or later, you will have to stand on your own two feet anyway. Your team is not going to hold your hand for long.

Great teams usually make new hires feel welcome. If you are lucky, your team will arrange something to help you feel like part of the group. Even if it is just a call or an email with instructions on what to do next, you should never feel completely on your own. In the rare event that you do find yourself completely isolated, proceed as follows:

1. Reach out to your boss and whichever team members you have met before. Contact them by phone (or by email). Tell them that you have successfully "landed" and would be willing to offer support with whatever needs attention.

2. Send a short introductory email to your entire team unless someone else from HR or your team has introduced you within twenty-four hours of the induction session.

Keep in mind that this is the exception, rather than the rule. However, as this still happens every so often, I find it worthwhile to emphasize that sitting and waiting for people to approach you is not acceptable. There is not much more for you to do at this point. Keep networking and wait for the support requests to flow into your inbox. Trust me, it will happen.

IT EQUIPMENT DOES NOT WORK

Consider yourself lucky if you do not have any technical issues when you start your new job. Certain hiccups should be expected. There are all sorts of problems that you may encounter, including:

- No access to the intranet for unknown reasons

- Limited access rights to the time reporting system

- Email reception only at the office, not remotely (e.g., from home)

- Mobile phone (if applicable) not being operable for at least twenty-four hours

This can be a frustrating first experience. Your team members will understand that you have technical issues that you are working to resolve, and this is exactly what you should spend your time working on.

FIRST WEEK ACTION PLAN

For those who need more specific guidance on what to do when they are just starting their new job, I have sketched out what potential actions could be taken throughout the first week. For the sake of this exercise, let's assume that you start on a Monday and the first day is primarily spent on the induction event. Once again, remember what you are trying to accomplish in your first days with the company (Figure 2).

 Making yourself known:
Introduce yourself using your self-introduction script/pitch.

 Showing interest:
Offer your help and project a strong willingness to work.

 Building your network:
Get to know people outside your team, incl. other administrative support staff.

 Getting up and running:
Solve any remaining problems, incl. IT issues, relocation, permits, etc.

 Familiarizing yourself with tools and systems:
Once you are working, there is little time to try things out. Learn about your company's resources to get the job done now.

Figure 2: First Week Objectives

Day	Action	Comment
Monday (1)	Attend induction event Meet the team (ongoing) Meet your mentor (if applicable) Send introductory email to boss (if not met in person)	Limited time available on the first day. Somebody is likely going to take care of you.
Tuesday (2)	Meet secretaries (and other administrative support staff) Finalize any potential follow-on tasks (e.g. upload CV to intranet)	Liaise with your administrative support staff. Do not leave seemingly minor tasks undone; get them out of the way quickly.
Wednesday (3)	Meet IT department	Meet the IT guys and make friends with them. Also try to solve issues you might have encountered already.
Thursday (4)	Meet other fellow juniors for lunch Ensure all pending issues have been resolved or escalated	Unless any other meaningful actions occur, touch base with the peers (e.g. those you met during the induction). Use this occasion to share first experiences.
Friday (5)	Meet team members (or manager/ mentor) for lunch	Chances are some senior practitioner will schedule a lunch with you. If not, make the suggestion yourself.

Table 2: First Week Action Plan

From this, we can derive a set of potential first week actions (Table 2). They should by no means set the boundaries of what you do. You should go beyond, if possible. Be the first at the office. Show initiative. Ask questions.

Obviously, you do not have to follow through on this. This is a recommendation, but one that has worked for many others before. Also note that any work deliverables to which you have been assigned should take priority.

KEY TAKEAWAYS

♦ Settle first. Spend all your effort on quickly getting up and running in your first week. Resolve remaining issues, learn about the company, and network as if your life depended on it.

- Don't try to impress at the induction event. Be a likeable participant and convey genuine interest. Avoid using the session as a personal platform, as this can put people off and word will likely get back to your team.

- Meet your colleagues but don't cling to them. Someone in your team will support your onboarding process. Remember that he or she has a day job and babysitting is not part of it.

- Don't give in to early frustration. The start might be different from your expectations (e.g., lack of team availability, poor IT equipment, different work from what you expected). Trust that the situation will get better and keep learning.

- Schedule key tasks. Make a first week action plan based on your objectives (e.g., make yourself known, show interest, build your network, get up and running, and familiarize yourself with tools and systems). This will help you structure your first few days and keep you on track.

[4]

The People You Meet
When You Start

*"You can make more friends in two months by becoming
interested in other people than you can in two years by trying
to get other people interested in you."*

Dale Carnegie,
How to Win Friends and Influence People

B Y NOW, IT SHOULD be clear that when you start working in
a new organization, you need to quickly develop an internal
network. Figure 3 provides an overview of the different actors in a typical corporation that you should be aware of. It is important to note that each of the different areas can potentially consist
of more than one person. Given that your capacity is limited, you
will need to focus your networking efforts on those that matter right
from the start. Clearly, those with a say in your career should be your
target, as well as those you met during the interview phase.

In this chapter, we will focus solely on those you are likely to meet
at the very beginning and on a day-to-day basis. We will talk through

the different stakeholders, specifically your manager, your immediate team, and, somewhat more broadly, the rest of the company. For each, we will look at the person or group's role, typical challenges, perception, and expectations of you, along with ways to keep everyone happy.

You will notice that we are not going to address the mentoring topic in this chapter. We have separated this from this discussion, as it deserves to be elaborated on in significantly more depth in Chapter 12. In addition, we will only address the rest of the company in brief. A more in-depth discussion, including specific actors, follows in Chapter 11.

YOUR MANAGER

ROLE

Your manager is usually in charge of some distinct part of the company, potentially an entire business unit or function. He or she is

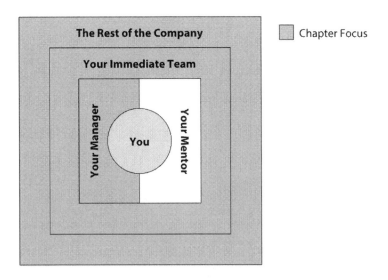

Figure 3: Networking Landscape

also responsible for managing his or her own cost center. As such, he or she is one of the most important players in your network. Your manager will be the one standing between you and good learning opportunities, either in the shape of challenging work assignments or training sessions. Ultimately, you also need his or her support when it comes to promotions.

CHALLENGES

A team lead is measured against hard, quantifiable objectives. While focus might differ depending on the role of your team within the organization, key criteria often include some type of profitability metric.

In addition, a team leader needs to ensure that the people under his or her supervision are qualified for the job. Any slack in the system is detrimental to overall performance as well as team morale. The latter is the second major concern for a team leader: how to keep the team engaged (if not happy). Your manager will have to strike a fine balance to keep everyone accountable and on target while successfully building a true team.

PERCEPTION OF YOU

To your manager, you are both an opportunity and a burden, but you have been hired for a reason. For now, you are expected to be able to quickly add value. In other words, there is hope that you will enrich the team to meet or exceed the team's objectives.

At the same time, there is the burden that you represent. You are a cost and a risk. On Day 1, there is only a slight chance that you will be truly valuable. Occasionally, there are junior-level resources that deliver exceptional work from Day 1 without much supervision. However, that is not the rule. More often than not, the company has to invest in juniors through proper onboarding, which ultimately is the responsibility of your manager and his or her team.

EXPECTATIONS OF YOU

Chances are that you are not the first junior member your manager has had to integrate into the team. He or she knows the challenges and is aware that there will be a learning curve before you can become a true asset. However, in order to make this happen quickly, you are expected to be willing to learn and go the extra mile when need be. Finally, no one feels hurt if you also show a bit of gratitude to those people providing you with this opportunity, including your manager.

KEY ACTIONS FOR YOU

Keep your manager happy by being willing to suck it up for a certain amount of time. Also, don't restrict yourself to those things that you think you are interested in. Early in your career, you don't fully know all of the great opportunities that exist.

One thing is certain. Things can be tough in the beginning. Whatever the challenges may be, persist. Help build the team, grow the business,[9] and seek ways to work toward your manager's goals. Try to understand what keeps him or her up at night.[10] Anticipate potential issues quickly and offer solutions. Nobody likes to hear a list of problems. Come up with potential remedies and offer to take care of the implementation thereof (yes, volunteer).

YOUR IMMEDIATE TEAM

ROLE

Your immediate team will become your new home on Day 1. As such, this is your new family for the months or years to come. You will likely work together in multiple capacities. Of course, professional work is the cornerstone of the relationship. However, expect to work together on corporate social responsibilities as well as team-building activities.

CHALLENGES

The main challenge for your team is to reach its goals. These could be sales or recruiting targets, employee retention, employee engagement...the list goes on and on. This really depends on the specific part of the company. In working towards accomplishing the team's objectives, it will be critical to keep everyone engaged.

In addition, some colleagues may have one eye on their next promotion. In a perfect world, this should not cause any issues, but wherever people with potentially conflicting interests mingle (i.e., most organizations are fixed pies, meaning people can only be promoted if there are vacant positions), you can expect tension. Don't be surprised if you find a certain degree of dysfunction within your team. Not everyone may be working collaboratively with one another. Often, the reasons for that may be found in the past and have nothing to do with you.

PERCEPTION OF YOU

When you are new and relatively inexperienced, you will initially be a burden to some members of the team. Perhaps someone will have been assigned to initially act as your so-called buddy to take you under his or her wing. Training a new hire takes time, but most people understand that you will become an asset to the team if they can properly onboard you.

By and large, new colleagues are always welcome, because they usually add resources and help the wider team get more work done. At the same time, you should be aware that there might be people who regard you as an easy target to assign tasks to. Some believe that an important part of one's development is doing "shitty" jobs; after all, they might have had to go through the same thing in the past. Others simply want an easy way out of their responsibilities and will take advantage of you. Unfortunately, you can find people with such views at all levels, and there is very little you can do to identify them up front. In the beginning, you simply have to deal with it professionally by delivering the work that is expected of you.

EXPECTATIONS OF YOU

Similar to your manager, your team expects you to work toward the common goals set for the group. In addition, they will want you to become a valuable member of the team and someone with whom to have fun. After all, you spend a great deal of time together.

KEY ACTIONS FOR YOU

From Day 1, make an effort to get to know your team. Join them for coffee or lunch, and try to understand their roles. Also, do not feel shy joining in conversations in the office. Have your ears open and show that you want to be part of the group. Also, make yourself heard with respect to actual work. Go the extra mile and produce exceptional deliverables.

Be conscious of the fact that there may be people who will try to take advantage of you. Do not let this stop you from giving your full effort. Instead, help these types of people once, and then stick to the "cool guys." There will almost certainly be people on the team who treat you more fairly. Stay close to them and seek ways to support them going forward. It is easier to turn down requests when you are busy with other important tasks. For additional information on declining tasks, please refer to Chapter 17.

THE REST OF THE COMPANY

ROLE

The rest of company represents exactly what the term implies. It pays to have good, collaborative relations with people in other parts of the company; but, by and large, the rest of the company's significance to you as a junior-level resource is limited.

CHALLENGES

The challenges for people in other parts of the organization are manifold. This depends on the specific part of the company, as well as the overall size and structure of the company, but also, more generally, the industry. As such, there is nothing for you to address specifically.

PERCEPTION OF YOU

Unless you have already gained some modicum of respect or a reputation, people in other parts of the company will have no perception of you whatsoever. Most organizations are so large that it is difficult enough to keep track of developments within one's own business unit or function. Anything beyond that is often difficult to comprehend or keep track of, to say the least.

EXPECTATIONS OF YOU

Given that people usually do not know you, they do not have specific expectations of you. At the very least, they do not want you to put the company's reputation at risk in any way.

KEY ACTIONS FOR YOU

Despite its relatively low level of importance to your early career, don't discard the rest of the company altogether. Slowly establishing a network throughout the organization can help you get insights that others can't.

While easier said than done, you should focus on building relationships with people in areas that are potentially compatible with your own area of expertise, with those you have come into professional contact with already, or with whomever seems most useful for your promotional path (see Chapter 11 for further details on how to network effectively).

KEY TAKEAWAYS

♦ Understand the networking landscape and how individual stakeholders (or groups thereof) relate to you.

♦ Nurture key relationships. By virtue of just starting out, there are people who will connect with you. Put significant effort into bonding with them. This will lay the groundwork for months or years to come.

♦ Put yourself in the shoes of your colleagues. Try to see things from their perspective. Recognize their challenges and seek ways to accommodate them accordingly.

[5]

Delivering Great Work

"I do the very best I know how—the very best I can; and I mean to keep on doing so until the end."

Abraham Lincoln

ALL THE PREPARATION AND social skills in the world are irrelevant if you are not able to get the job done. Delivering high-quality work is essential in all career tracks. It is better to have a socially awkward delivery monkey on the team than someone who works the room like a politician but whose work is unreliable.

The trouble for those starting out is a lack of experience. Without guidance, it is difficult to understand what high-quality deliverables actually are. Likewise, not all people you are supposed to support should be treated equally. However, as a junior, who are you to know the difference? By the end of this chapter, you will have a clear idea of what is required and how to make it happen.

We will start by looking at the different types of stakeholders ("clients") with whom you are going to come into contact. For each, we will highlight the key differences and levels of importance. After-

49

ward, we will take a closer look at what quality actually means when delivering any type of job.

Finally, we will conclude the chapter with some pointers on how to produce typical examples of deliverables, including presentations and Excel models, in addition to making a case for learning Visual Basic for Applications (VBA).

YOUR CLIENTS

Throughout this book, I refer to serving clients. This is clearly consulting lingo, but I believe there are few things more appropriate for juniors than perceiving others as potential clients. A client is anyone you are working for. Whether an internal or external client (e.g., a customer), it doesn't matter. What does matter, is how you relate to them. Let's look at each separately and shed some light on how to serve them best.

INTERNAL CLIENTS

At many times, but definitely early in your career, your main client will most often be one of your internal senior colleagues, perhaps your manager. Some would even argue, "The most important client is the internal client." Do not let your standards slip; providing support to internal clients can make or break careers.

Internal clients can be manifold, and, depending on seniority, your priorities may have to change instantly. After all, it makes a difference (career-wise) if you provide support to the head of the company, your manager, some peer-level resource or other back-office staff. Some will have a say in your future development, job opportunities, and promotions. Others won't. Keep that in mind, especially when being confronted with ad hoc requests, and manage them accordingly, noting that general manners and respect should guide your behavior at all times.

It is also important to recognize that changing priorities may be more common when working for internal clients. Your colleagues typically have a better understanding of what you will be able to accomplish if you are simply pushed a little more. That's just the way it is. You will end up juggling different balls in the air, and you will have to become good at it. For more guidance on how to push back when you have to, refer to Chapter 17.

In addition, you may be asked to support internal matters that are not necessarily related to your core job. These may include brand building (e.g., marketing), business development (e.g., proposals, research), talent development (e.g., training, recruiting), team building (e.g., team events), or other initiatives. Do not categorically rule out supporting those. Instead, volunteer for some of these jobs. You should consider these pieces of work as stepping-stones to future opportunities by showcasing your skills and building your professional brand.

EXTERNAL CLIENTS

In some career tracks, you will have exposure to external clients (e.g., customers). However, unless you are in a direct sales role, internal clients will still be more relevant for juniors just starting out. This is not to say that you should seek out shortcuts when working with external clients. Based on experience, some managers will try to limit a junior's direct client exposure in the beginning. As such, you will work for your manager rather than the external client.

Of course, there are always exceptions to the rule. You might have colleagues who end up conducting client interviews right from the start. Such situations are the exception and are likely borne out of necessity, not particular skills on the part of the junior resource.

Similar to internal clients, there is not a "typical" external client. There are many different types and they greatly depend on your industry. Based on the circumstances, all client personnel have the potential to make or break your prospects. Accordingly, all of them should matter to you, irrespective of their level in the hierarchy, because what they all have in common is your professional relationship toward them. Be humble and seek to provide value every single day. This is the golden rule of business.

A good relationship with the client is important, but ultimately, it doesn't matter how well one can connect with a client on a personal basis, because when "the shit hits the fan," you will still take the blame. Therefore, carefully consider what you say to whom, when, and how, even during more informal gatherings. You are a product or service provider, and as such, you must uphold the highest standards in terms of confidentiality and professionalism at all times.

Having gained an understanding of the different clients and challenges you may face, let's look at how you can actually deliver great work.

WHAT ARE HIGH-QUALITY DELIVERABLES?

First off, what are deliverables? Anything that someone will receive from you. This can range from a short email in a business context or a discussion document to financial models and in-depth presentations.

Most of my consulting clients have a very clear idea of what quality means to them. Essentially, quality boils down to three aspects: accuracy, timeliness, and design (Figure 4). Get these consistently right and you will be off to a promising career.

Let's review these quality components in order of their importance to your clients.

- **Accuracy:** Whatever you deliver, it has to be accurate.[11] Internal and external clients alike often do not have time to check your final outputs in detail. While they will do common sense checks, they also have to trust your competence. Before submitting anything to the client, in-

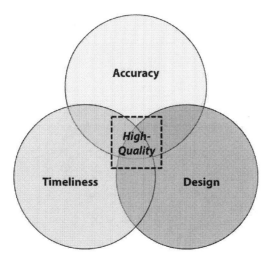

Figure 4: Quality Components in Deliverables

cluding intermittent updates, conduct an in-depth re-view of your own work. For starters, you should focus on spelling as well as the accuracy of any calculations made. For correct spelling, make sure your language settings have been applied consistently throughout the deliver-able (e.g., UK vs. US English). When reviewing calcula-tions, focus on totals and subtotals, if there are any. This is the quickest method to spot errors rather than calcu-lating everything again.

Remember, paying attention to details is crucial. Im-agine buying a car and finding that the rear mirror is missing one screw. How confident would you be that the rest of the car, including the brakes, was manufactured more thoroughly? The same holds true for deliverables. Details reflect on the quality of the total work product.

- **Timeliness:** Preparation time for deliverables varies, but the vast amount of deliverables has one thing in common—you wish you had more time at your disposal. Regardless of how much time you end up having, you will have to meet the expected deadline set by your client. If this is not feasible, you should flag that immediately, ideally up front, as managing expectations is key. No one likes surprises.

Therefore, avoid agreeing on timelines that you cannot realistically work within. If you are requested to work toward such a timeline, highlight which potential changes in scope could be made. However, once agreed, you have to meet the deadline. No exception. There is no excuse for not meeting an agreed deadline. If you need additional support, reach out to your network. Chances are, someone has the capacity to help out, or others might have done something similar before and can provide guidance that will speed up your own work. Don't feel too proud to ask for help. Nobody can do everything all by him- or herself. If all else fails, let your manager know of your constraints promptly.

- **Design:** When speaking about getting the design right, we are usually referring to design standards and aesthetics. Now I know from my consulting clients, as well as those interviewed for this book, that there are vast differences in terms of the design quality of deliverables. Many people in larger organizations focus exclusively on content, thereby forgetting that how you package things also matters.

  For you, this means that you can easily stand out. First, ensure full compliance with the standard design principles set out by your company. This includes the usage of the standard template and consistent use of the provided color palette. Second, produce only visually appealing deliverables. As with anything, "beauty" always lies in the eye of the beholder. Thus, what looks good to you might not necessarily appeal to your (internal or external) client. Expect multiple iterations, particularly when working with more senior colleagues. Don't get married to your deliverable or take any feedback or reiterations personally. Whatever makes the client happy is the way to go. If that means replacing blue circles with green triangles, go ahead and change them accordingly.

Knowing what to generally watch out for when producing deliverables, we will now take a more in-depth look at how to actually get the job done.

PRODUCING HIGH-QUALITY DELIVERABLES

Let's get a bit more specific about the different types of deliverables that you are likely to encounter. To begin with, I will reiterate the importance of structuring your thinking prior to actually working on any task. We will then highlight the most common types of deliverables as well as common pitfalls.

GET YOUR THINKING RIGHT

Regardless of the request at hand, before you start working, you should step back and think through your approach to the problem. As a matter of fact, this is probably the single most important step to creating any effective work output. Unfortunately, it is often omitted.

The most common approach in a business environment is based on the Minto pyramid concept. Barbara Minto, an ex-McKinsey consultant, proposes structuring thoughts as a pyramid. Thus, the main idea is on top, while supporting arguments follow underneath.

To avoid paraphrasing what Minto has already made available, the key advice here is for you to get her book. At a minimum, do some online research to thoroughly understand the concept. It might be a dry topic to deal with, but it will help you throughout your career in structuring your thoughts and communicating in an effective, compelling fashion. For further resources on structured thinking, see the Appendix.

Typical Applications and Usage

Certain types of roles require special software applications. Human resources may have their own recruiting platform, finance might quarrel with SAP, while sales potentially do the heavy lifting with a customer relationship management (CRM) tool. However, in most business environments, Microsoft PowerPoint, Excel, and Word (apart from your email client) are the most commonly used programs organization-wide. Regardless of your area, you are likely to work with any of the three aforementioned applications on a daily basis. Make sure you know the ins and outs of all three applications. If need be, work through online tutorials before starting your work or on weekends once you identify any room for improvement.

Getting From Task Reception to Deliverable

It would be beyond the scope of this book to discuss in detail how all types of deliverables should best be approached. Instead, below you will find a brief overview of common challenges, along with a 10-step high-level process guiding you from task reception to final delivery.

The Challenges

Based on my experience, a mixture of different factors represent the key challenges for junior resources in delivering work, including:

- Unclear scope (i.e., what is included and what is excluded)

- Last minute requests (i.e., limited time)

- Changing requirements of the deliverable

- Limited input from subject matter experts (SMEs)

- Additional deliverable requests

These challenges are of little concern individually. However, when taken collectively, things become tricky. Therefore, you will seek to cover yourself early in the process by locking in as many items as possible. The approach that works best to accomplish this is explained next.

THE 10-STEP PROCESS THAT WORKS

No matter how big or small the task, you should follow a standard process when you produce any type of deliverable. "Highly successful people are all presenting a very consistent message. Their success is due in part to their ability to focus on what is in front of them. They are aware of the bigger picture, but their focus is honed onto the task in hand," finds performance coach Simon Hartley.[12] A structured approach can simplify the consistent development of successful deliverables. Clearly, the amount of work put into each and every step varies depending on the type of work. Follow the sequence (see Figure 5) and consider adopting it in your daily routine.

1. Receive request: Be open and try to show interest when you receive a new request. Obviously, you want to avoid jumping on each and every opportunity. Be somewhat selective and don't be afraid to mention potential capacity constraints. If these are flagged up front, your client might seek out additional support or consider alternative options.

2. Confirm understanding of request: Once you have agreed to take on a certain task, ensure that you have a

Step		Comment	Involvement
1	**Receive Request**	Be somewhat selective. Don't jump on every opportunity. Flag any potential issues upfront.	You
2	**Confirm Understanding**	Avoid any uncertainties. Clarify requirements and intended timeline before starting your work.	You & Manager
3	**Think Through Approach**	There are usually multiple approaches. Step back and think of the most practical one.	You
4	**Prepare Draft**	Go low tech. Step back from your machine, and prepare a rough draft using pen and paper.	You
5	**Confirm Approach**	Get feedback on your approach and agree on how to proceed best. Achieving agreement is critical.	You & Manager
6	**Execute Agreed Approach**	Execute. Execute. Execute.	You
7	**Provide Update**	Inform your manager in person or by email, share your latest version, and request feedback.	You & Manager
8	**Incorporate Feedback**	Visibly include the feedback points.	You
9	**Finalize & Review**	Dot the i's and cross the t's. Check spelling, alignment, totals and subtotals, etc.	You
10	**Deliver Document**	Deliver on time – not before. Ensure your work is top quality. Check wording if you deliver by email.	You

Figure 5: 10-Step Deliverable Production Process

good understanding of what you are required to do. You want to be completely clear about the scope of the work and the intended timeline. If in doubt, it is always better to ask.

3. Think through the approach: When you are clear about what the desired output should be, spend some time considering different approaches for how to get there. Some tasks will be straightforward, while others will not. In the latter case, there will rarely be one perfect approach. Choose the one that has the least constraints or downsides.

4. Prepare draft structure: Once you have decided the angle from which to tackle the problem, prepare a draft outline of your approach. It is a good idea to step back from your

machine and use pen and paper for your thought process at this stage.

5. Confirm your approach: Align with your client in terms of the approach that is to be taken. This step is vital, and it is in your self-interest not to skip it. Even if the task is a no-brainer, be transparent about what you are planning to do. For more complex tasks, present your initial thoughts and draft structure, and validate both of them with your client. While doing so, be open to criticism. Don't get too hung up on your initial plan.

6. Execute the agreed approach: Once your client agrees with your approach, set out to implement it. Do not go into execution mode before you have achieved overall alignment with your client. The only exception may be your client telling you to get started despite some uncertainties or when you are aware of significant risks if the start is delayed.

7. Provide updates: Do not become a hermit. Keep your client in the loop regarding your progress and flag potential, previously unanticipated, issues. At a minimum, provide at least one intermittent update to your client for every deliverable. This update should serve to inform about the current state of the project (roughly 60–70 percent complete) and allow for potential feedback from the client. *Note*: If you are working for important external clients, your manager should be involved throughout the process. You will want to ensure that your manager has reviewed whatever will be shared with third parties.

8. Incorporate feedback: If you have received some constructive feedback, amend your deliverable accordingly.

Do not be selective as to what to include. Your judgment on these points is not required, as your client will look specifically for earlier feedback points upon receiving the final version.

9. Finalize and review deliverable: Complete any remaining parts of the deliverable, and conduct an in-depth review, including:

    –   Alignment of all components (if applicable, such as boxes, headlines, and margins)

    –   Consistent use of font style (type and size)

    –   Spelling

    –   Naming conventions

    –   All abbreviations written out at least once

    –   Pages numbered according to standards

    –   Correct subtotals and totals in calculations

    –   Printability of the files (if applicable), including correct labeling of margins (date, page number of total number of pages, client logo, etc.)

10. Deliver the final document: When you deliver the final document, maintain the highest quality standard. Do not ruin your hard work by presenting it in a less than ideal way. Content is important, but the quality of presentation ranks very highly too. That means, if it concerns an important external recipient, you may need to resort to other external service providers (e.g., printing, binding).

Armed with a standard process to develop most deliverables, you will be well on your way to excellent job performance. Before moving on to other topics, let me provide you with some additional guidance.

First, I will share some best practices for producing two very common work outputs: business presentations and Excel models. In closing, you will learn about a useful, often underrated skill that you should consider acquiring—a good command of VBA.

6 Steps to Building Effective Presentations

One of the most frequently used tools in today's office environment is PowerPoint. In fact, being able to create PowerPoint presentations is what some people acknowledge as the only valuable addition from business consultants. Naturally, I disagree. However, I understand that consultants are usually pretty good at building compelling business presentations. Though this is not a handbook for consultants, I believe that there is value in explaining in more detail how anyone—regardless of industry—can level up their PowerPoint game.

Whatever important message consultants need to express is likely put on slides. The "death by PowerPoint" notion does not exist as far as consultants are concerned. In fact, on the contrary, more people should become skilled in building business presentations. After all, "It's not the tool, it's how the tool is used," say management experts Jay Barney and Trish Clifford.[13] Presentations, if structured correctly, can actually be very effective communication vehicles. I have seen some of my clients having a hard time getting individuals to buy-in from various parts of their organization because they had not figured out how to communicate in a compelling fashion. Facts are one thing, but the right packaging is also essential.

How should you build business presentations? While there may be more iterations depending on the recipient, the fundamental production process should consist of the following six steps (also see Figure 6).

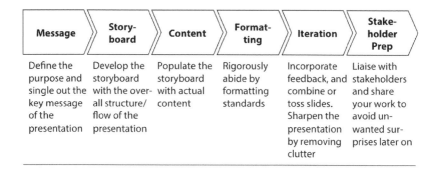

Message	Story-board	Content	Format-ting	Iteration	Stake-holder Prep
Define the purpose and single out the key message of the presentation	Develop the storyboard with the over-all structure/flow of the presentation	Populate the storyboard with actual content	Rigorously abide by formatting standards	Incorporate feedback, and combine or toss slides. Sharpen the presentation by removing clutter	Liaise with stakeholders and share your work to avoid un-wanted sur-prises later on

Figure 6: 6-Step Slide Production Process

1. Define the purpose and single out the key message. What is the purpose of the presentation? What is your key message? The more specific you can be here, the more concrete your first draft of the presentation will be.

2. Develop the storyboard. To communicate convincingly requires being able to tell a story because the best message can fail to be received—or even backfire—if not properly presented in a convincing, logical fashion. To accomplish that, you should work with so-called "storyboards."

   Basically, this is an approach that structures a presentation like a book with multiple chapters. Each chapter is represented by at least one slide and one meaningful headline (strapline). As a complete "narrative," the storyboard should make sense. Thus, it should be clear, coherent, and ordered in a logical manner, such as chronologically (think phases or process steps), departmentally (think business units or functions), or geographically (think markets).

In practice, there are different ways of developing a storyboard. A practical approach is to use Post-it notes. Capturing each idea on a separate note makes it very easy to reshuffle the pieces until you have found an ideal structure. You can see an example of this process in Figure 7, showing my own efforts to write my first book.

3. Populate the storyboard with content. With your storyboard in place, you will then have to add content on each page. The key is to be very selective in terms of what to include. Whatever text box, image, graph, etc., you use should clearly add value. There should be a reason for having everything in there. Also, ensure that each slide really has one key message. If you can't convincingly answer your potential audience's "So what?" question, then amend or remove that slide. Obviously, different people have different styles; so if you know someone is really into details, then provide as much information (if just in the appendix) as possible. Otherwise, keep it to the bare minimum.

   You should always adjust your presentation depending on the audience. Do not simply stick to your personal preference. It is a good starting point, but the bait is supposed to suit the fish, not the angler. *Note:* In this step, you may also want to consider what parts of previous presentations you can leverage. You do not have to reinvent the wheel. At times, slight adjustments will do just fine.

4. Rigorously abide by presentation standards. At the very least, ensure that you are in line with the following:

   – Clear overall message of the presentation

- Meaningful titles
- Most important messages come first
- One key message per slide, and certainly no more than two (unless your audience has a liking for cluttered pages in font size eight)
- Consistent structure of text, i.e., all bullet points to start with a verb (same tense)
- Text and images/graphs support each other, (e.g., readers may be pointed to specific aspects of the visuals)
- Minimal amount of text
- Consistent structure of slides, i.e., similar layout
- Repetitive phrases should be avoided
- Pages that are similar in nature may be combined to avoid repetition

5. Iterate. Iterate. Iterate. Regardless of how hard you try when structuring your first draft, you will inevitably change your presentation numerous times. You will combine slides and toss out others. Feedback from other people, as well as your own gut feeling, will help you develop a presentation that is both compelling and sharp. You should conduct a final and very strict review of what needs to be included. Get rid of any clutter. Cut away until you are left with the bare essentials. This will not only reduce the size of the presentation, but will also sharpen the message.

6. Prepare your stakeholders. Once you have completed your presentation, liaise with key stakeholders and share

Figure 7: Storyboarding for my first book, *The Aspiring Advisor*

your work. It is crucially important that you not surprise your audience. Even if you assume that they will likely agree, chances are they won't if they're caught off guard. Therefore, never publish any presentation unless you have secured buy-in from your key stakeholders.

For additional resources for creating effective presentations, see the Appendix.

Again, don't try to reinvent the wheel when designing presentations. For starters, get a copy of a "presentation timesaver" file from your company (otherwise, use Google to find publicly available examples). More often than not, you will be able to at least draw from them for some inspiration.

When you are new to an organization, you should also ask your colleagues for example presentations (even on different topics). This will allow you to get a better feel for what style and structure they prefer.

HOW TO DEVELOP GOOD EXCEL MODELS

There are plenty of resources out there concerning how to get the most out of Excel, and most of these resources are online. The following section will not try to paraphrase all of the content that is already out there (for detailed resources, refer to the Appendix). Instead, this section will provide some guidance on how to build good Excel models based on years of practical experience. We will cover two key questions that you should always ask yourself before building a model, a detailed review of different types of Excel models, and five modeling design principles with which you should comply.

Before we get into it, don't be intimidated by the word "model". I understand that not every career track requires building Excel models. However, almost all roles these days require a solid command of Excel. The principles laid out in the following section apply to any type of work with Excel. Thus, you will benefit in certain ways, even if you never develop a financial model in Excel.

TWO KEY QUESTIONS TO GET YOU STARTED

Just like any other request that you agreed to work on, don't rush ahead and start building an Excel model right away. Step back for a moment and think through the task conceptually. The following questions are key.

What is the purpose of the model? Often the model will be simple and used only for some quick analysis. A core data set, simple formulae (e.g., VLOOKUP), and pivot tables might suffice.

Who is the recipient? You will have to consider both formatting and usability depending on who is going to access the file. If the model is for your own use (i.e., other people will not see it), then whatever works for you is just fine. If you are only asked by your manager to "come up with a number," then nothing fancy is required. If the output is to be formally handed over to an external party, then a top-notch model is what you will want to go for.

Based on your answers to the above questions, you will have a fairly good understanding of the scope of the model that you will have to develop. The following Excel model maturity levels will provide further guidance.

COMMON EXCEL MODEL MATURITY LEVELS

Depending on both the complexity of the matter at hand as well as the intended recipient of the model, we can distinguish between three different Excel model maturity levels (see Table 3). Each level fulfills a slightly different objective, comes with more or less overall workbook complexity (e.g., color-coding, annotations), and requires a different degree of workbook protection (e.g., certain cells or sheets may be blocked from being modified or even viewed).

Level 1 represents the simplest model. Each higher level combines the qualities from the preceding level in addition to further elements. Thus, Level 2 is a slightly more sophisticated extension of Level 1. When you actually build the model, you will have to work your way up. You should initially focus on getting the data right before wasting time on formatting the nitty-gritty details.

Let's review each level in more detail.

	Level 1	Level 2	Level 3
User	You	Internal client	External client
Objective	Accurate data	Easy to review	Easy to use
Workbook Complexity	Low/Medium	Medium	High
Workbook Protection	Low	Low/Medium	Medium/High

Table 3: Excel Model Maturity Levels

LEVEL 1

- Intended user: You (or peer-level colleagues)

- Objective: Accurate data

- Workbook complexity: Low/Medium

- Workbook protection: Low

- Description: Intended for your own use. Nobody else will work with the model. Focus on getting the analysis right. It does not need to be fancy. However, remember that you might need to update the model in the future. Hence, apply modeling standards wherever possible.

- Key considerations:

  - What is the logic within the model? Does it make sense?

  - Is the data clean and relevant (e.g., fairly recent information, sufficiently large sample size)?

  - What will I have to calculate, and what will this mean for the model structure?

LEVEL 2

- Intended user: Internal client (e.g., your manager)

- Objective: Easy to review

- Workbook complexity: Medium

- Workbook protection: Low/Medium

- Description: This type of model is to be used by someone in your company (e.g., your manager). Your manager will most likely have a solid command of Excel. Accordingly, focus not so much on ease of use, but on enabling others to review and validate the accuracy of the analysis.

- Key considerations:

    - Can other people understand the mechanics of the model? Ensure the structure of the file makes sense (i.e., is ordered logically).

    - Have you documented all assumptions and data sources? The more specific and complete an overview that you provide here, the easier it is for others to reconcile your work.

    - Have you removed clutter? Anything unnecessary, including data sheets and irrelevant analyses, should be removed or sidelined temporarily. Just like in an appendix of a book, put all the nonessential information and references in the back.

    - Is your workbook easy to navigate? Can another person immediately access the key output sheets? Just because you start working from a data input sheet does not mean that output sheets featuring the result of the analysis have to come last. Rearrange the order so it makes sense for the user.

LEVEL 3

- Intended user: External client (or other senior person)
- Objective: Easy to use
- Workbook complexity: High
- Workbook protection: Medium/High

- Description: This model is to be used by someone external, or a senior person in your company who might not be particularly experienced using Excel (this should be your working assumption). Accordingly, the model should be accurate and easy to use for all experience levels. One memorable client of mine always requested that I make things "donkey-proof." Make the presentation as easy to navigate as possible by using consistent formatting, color-coding, and annotations (where necessary), and ensure that it is impossible to break the model itself.

- Key considerations:

  - Have you included a cover sheet? Just like in a presentation, add a simple yet visually pleasing cover page for your model.

  - Do you have a table of contents guiding the user? This sheet should provide a complete overview of how the workbook is structured. For ease of use, ideally, you should also add links to the different sheets here.

  - Can someone break the model single-handedly? Apply proper protection of worksheets, cells, and ranges to prevent your client from accidentally corrupting the model.

  - For larger workbooks, have you included and validated some type of dashboard incorporating information from several output sheets? Given that most clients are short on time, an overview with the key metrics can be highly valuable to them.

– Is the file ready to be printed? You will have to change the print settings and prepare correct margins (e.g., page number, date, title).

– Does the file open on the first tab? To ensure that the recipient is not going to be lost right away by being on Tab 17, Cell W301, save the file while you are showing the first tab (ideally, cell A1). This will ensure that your file opens on the first tab in the upper left-hand corner.

MODELING DESIGN PRINCIPLES MAKING YOUR LIFE EASIER

Regardless of the complexity of your model, there are certain modeling "dos and don'ts" by which you should abide. They will make your life easier when updating the model with fresh data and will also accommodate third-party use.

Remember the following five points, and you will be well on your way to Excel model mastery.

• **Don't hard code:** Never type numbers as part of formulas directly into cells. Not only will it be hard for you to update, but the model will also be error-prone and next to impossible for others to reconcile.

• **Always refer to one source cell:** Especially when running through different scenarios, you will want to see the effect of changing key parameters. Make sure that these parameters (e.g., sales) need to be changed manually only once. Using references to one source cell, the rest of the model should update itself automatically.

• **Apply formatting standards:** Make it a habit to be consistent in how you format your models. Just like any other document you create, an Excel model should be formatted consistently.

- **Separate data input and output using different sheets:**
  I recommend always having at least two sheets in each
  model, namely input and output. The first captures the
  data you have received or collated, while the second
  performs calculations and displays some results. (*Note*:
  It should be obvious that you can have multiple output
  sheets.) Make this a habit even for small analyses that
  only you will have to work with.

- **Do not play around with the source data:** Keep it clean.
  Don't change the structure by adding additional col-
  umns or subtotals. If you need to rework the data to
  make it useful for your analysis, arrange this conversion
  on a separate sheet (think of a sheet translating the original data set to something more useful). This will make
  your life easier when you receive an updated data set
  from your client.

Unfortunately, there are no resources that my colleagues and I
can wholeheartedly recommend when it comes to Excel modeling.
More often than not, you will have to start from a simple Google
search. This book comes with bonus material, including a curated
list of the most useful Excel shortcuts and formulas. To get free access, visit GotTheJobNowWhat.com/bonus.

VBA: The Competence That Will Simplify Your Work Life

Apart from learning how to produce specific deliverables, you should
do yourself a favor and learn how to use VBA. VBA, which is short for
Visual Basic for Applications, is a programming language developed
by Microsoft. It can be used across the Microsoft Office suite. For
example, in consulting, its usage is most common in Excel, but it has
very practical use in PowerPoint and Outlook too.

You do not have to be a tech genius to figure all of this out. I'm certainly not. I wrapped my head around this topic at some point simply because I had to. Most likely, you will eventually run into issues where VBA can help you save time or help you accomplish otherwise nearly impossible tasks.

The key benefit of VBA for me is automation. Whatever tasks you can think of, chances are, there is a way to automate it. Quickly filtering or sorting data based on a number of criteria? Generating custom reports from large Excel models? Sending hundreds of emails to different distribution lists directly out of Excel? Automatically producing presentations from Excel models? Merging 4,000 Word documents into one? The potential benefits of VBA are endless.

VBA has a bit of a steep learning curve, but it's not rocket science. There is plenty of material on the Internet that can help. You definitely do not have to reinvent the wheel. Most questions have been raised before, and you are unlikely to be the first to encounter certain problems that must be solved. If your firm offers VBA training courses, make an effort to participate. You will benefit from it either directly when using VBA on the job or indirectly when trying to make sense of someone else's Excel model.

KEY TAKEAWAYS

♦ Deliver only high-quality deliverables. Consistently produce accurate work in a timely and visually appealing fashion. Without good work, nothing else really matters.

♦ Be aware of the different clients you may be working with. Understand the different expectations and requirements for external and internal clients.

♦ Think about internal stakeholders first. Because these are key to a junior's early career, you have to satisfy internal clients before external ones.

♦ Be clear on what is expected of you. Avoid working on anything before you have agreed on the scope, timeline, and approach with your stakeholder.

♦ Be swift, but don't rush. Develop your deliverables systematically using standard routines, particularly for the most common deliverables in your area of work.

[6]

Mastering Email Communication

*"Email is familiar. It's comfortable. It's easy to use.
But it might just be the biggest killer of time
and productivity in the office today."*

Ryan Holmes

REGARDLESS OF YOUR INDUSTRY, you are going to use email a lot, so much so that you will soon begin to hate its mere existence. Unless you have been running a one-man show in a start-up, you will likely be overwhelmed at first. The sheer amount of email messages you will receive in most large organizations is likely greater than what you have experienced so far.

This chapter will show you some practical email management techniques, all of which you can implement instantly. Explanations will be brief. This is not a detailed how-to manual (don't expect screenshots!). The purpose of this chapter is to emphasize the importance of the subject matter and point you in the right direction. This is meant to help you see the big picture and focus on what works.

To begin with, I will establish common ground in terms of email communication in a business environment in general and from the perspective of a junior-level resource in particular. We will then look at adjustments you should make to your email client, including useful add-ons, to leverage its full power. After that, we will look at handling email from two different angles. First, I will show you some techniques to manage email within your email client. Second, we will delve into how to actually write business emails. We will conclude this chapter with an example email that drives home the concepts laid out previously.

I assume that your company is doing all its office work using the Microsoft Office suite. Hence, the email client would be Outlook. In the rare event that your company is not using Outlook, don't panic. You should still treat this section as critical, and do a quick search online on how to enable these settings in your particular email client.

Your Limitations

Let's get the bad news out of the way up front. Popular advice on how to manage emails is unlikely to work for most juniors just starting out. Contrary to what you may read elsewhere, you cannot switch to checking email only two or three times a day in most organizations. Likewise, switching off notifications will be impractical. As much as I would have liked to do so myself, I realized that it was simply not possible in my grade.

You will be bombarded with email that is both useful and seemingly superfluous. What could be discussed and solved in a quick call is often put into an email chain. Essentially, it frees up the sender, and puts the ball into someone else's court. This is not nice, especially since juniors have a hard time pushing back. Instead, you will be expected to act upon incoming email—quickly.

With this in mind, let's look at what you can do to make your life easier with respect to email.

Essential Outlook Settings

Anything out of the box is usually not what you will want to use. This also applies to your email client. Luckily, the settings do not need to be changed greatly. A handful of adjustments go a long way.

While there are plenty of interesting solutions to get more out of Outlook, we will focus on the important stuff here. This includes folder structure, time zones, and calendar access. Set this up right now or once you realize that you should have already done so.

Folder Structure

The basic folder structure of Outlook is not going to be useful for your purposes. Forget about studies analyzing the effectiveness of different methods for approaching email. Given the lack of proper search functionality in Outlook and the nature of work in most companies, you will want to have a minimal folder structure that reflects your working reality.

For a time, I played around with the Archive/Follow Up/Hold folder method, but I could not make it work for me, although I would have preferred it. The approach sounds very simplistic, and simplicity is great; but I felt that this was actually bogging me down and not helping me excel at managing emails.

As always, check close to home first. Reach out to fellow colleagues to see how they structured their inboxes. By and large, the most successful individuals in your companies will probably use something similar to the sample below.

Consider the following as a guide for setting up your folder structure:

- Separate internal and external topics (i.e., divide emails pertaining to your own company and external clients, if applicable)

- Create folders for all types of stakeholders that you deal with on a regular basis (e.g., different departments you exchange information with or project-based communication)

- Use subfolders for larger pieces of work, e.g.:

  - Project setup (e.g., onboarding documents, copies of the engagement contract)

  - Team administration (e.g., information about the project team, such as CVs and hours billed)

  - Project billing/costs (particularly where it pertains to external contractors)

  - Deliverables (e.g., key pieces of work to be delivered as part of a project)

  - Countries/business units/work streams (dependent on the nature of the work)

  - Reports (e.g., market data, industry reports, monthly sales reports)

  - Other (i.e., unanticipated topics)

- Consider creating folders for internal topics, such as:

  - Training/Learning & Development (e.g., training calendar, seminar information)

  - Performance Management (e.g., mentor communication)

  - HR Guidelines (e.g., employee handbook, policies)

- IT (e.g., guidelines, tutorials from the IT department, IT issues)

- Team Updates and Team Meetings (e.g., communication, presentations, discussion documents)

- Corporate Events (e.g., invitations)

- Expenses

- Vacation Requests

- AOB (Any Other Business) (i.e., random corporate messages that you do not delete right away and do not fit any other folder)

- Use numbering to improve the accessibility of folders in case the alphabetical order is not ideal. A quick fix to having one folder at the top is to add "A - [FOLDER NAME]"

- Create an "Archive/Sent Items" folder. I regularly move all sent items from the standard "Sent" folder to this specific folder for archiving purposes. This is done to free up space. Depending on your company, you may or may not need to do this.

More Time and Different Time Zones in Calendar

This might not appear relevant at first, but anyone who has ever worked in an internationally operating organization will appreciate the following changes to the Outlook calendar that allow you to expand the time frames shown in the calendar and add time zones. In addition, you might want to consider bookmarking www.everytimezone.com to give you quick access to all time zones and corresponding times in one easy-to-find place.

CALENDAR ACCESS

Assuming that this is your first job, you probably have not provided or been granted calendar access by anyone else in the past. However, going forward, the more widely accessible your team members' calendars are, the better it will be for everyone involved. Some colleagues might provide access right away, but don't expect this. Therefore, be proactive and adopt the following approach. It worked for others, and it will work for you.

First, check with your colleagues. Do they usually provide access to one another? If so, ask them to provide access to you, too. If this is uncommon, check with your boss and other relevant seniors to see if they would mind providing you access to their calendars. The key here is to only do this once you are asked to schedule the first meeting involving them. However well intended, anything else comes across as creepy.

At the very least, provide access to your calendar to other incoming juniors starting a month or so after you. You are basically their senior, and it is important to establish good habits when you can. This is the first time you can safely set a new standard.

THE LIFE-SAVING OUTLOOK ADD-ON

If you are willing to bend the rules in your favor, read on. Apart from being quick at navigating Outlook, you can go further and install what is probably the single most important add-on to consider: an enhanced Outlook search capability.

Few things worth having come for free. Similarly, the below add-ons come at a price. However, one-time license fees should not concern you if they can save you hours over the course of a year. There are a handful of options on the market. As of this writing, I would consider one of the following:

- Live Inbox, www.live-inbox.com

- Outlook Finder, www.outlookfinder.com

- Lookeen, www.lookeen.net

If you use Gmail privately, you will quickly notice how limited the search function in Outlook is. Neither I nor any of my colleagues with whom I have discussed this are satisfied with Outlook's search functionality. It is a running joke in most companies that you are better off asking your colleagues to resend certain emails before trying to search in Outlook for them—you won't find them anyway.

How Outlook Add-Ons Actually Work

Upon starting the add-on for the first time, your entire email client will be indexed. Depending on the amount of email you have stored, this may take some time. I have helped more senior colleagues set this up, and it easily took ten minutes or more. Thus, it is highly recommended to get this up and running from the start.

The Key Features You Will Use

While these add-ons come with some social media integration, you will most likely not be using them. Additional information pulled from social media platforms is nice to have, but it's not essential. In addition, some more or less in-depth analytics about your emailing behavior are usually provided. Most of this is interesting but clearly not relevant for now.

What are the relevant features then? Why am I mentioning these add-ons here? There are at least four benefits that can have a direct impact on your day-to-day work.

- **Finding email:** The add-ons help you find emails that others can't. You will get asked more often than expected to forward emails you sent in the past or to dig out an email on which you were only copied and shoot it over to your manager. Of course, all this has to happen as quickly as possible. There will be those people who cannot provide the same level of service. With any of these add-ons, you no longer have an excuse and will be able to find everything relatively easily. Search for any topic in subject lines and email bodies, or filter by sender. You can do this across the entire Outlook folder structure! Try this with basic Outlook . . . it was impossible when I last checked.

- **Finding files:** Oftentimes, what people are really after when searching for specific emails is a certain attachment. The add-ons mentioned above also come to the rescue in this situation. You can search for file types from a specific sender or by name. Managers will love you.

- **Retrieving contact information:** "Moritz, do you have the number from that marketing agency guy in Italy?" Being in the middle of something and being asked by your manager for a number that you definitely do not have on hand is terrible, especially while he is holding the telephone receiver in one hand. Don't let that happen. Using the Live Inbox add-on, search for any email from that respective person and see what contact details are provided. While often correct, make sure you do a sense check (it might be your own number). You might think that you could find the number just as easily yourself. After all, you have to look up some emails anyway. However, most signatures are not sent internally or as part of long email chains. Searching in the traditional way just isn't as reliable. An add-on might be the remedy. Remember, your manager is waiting.

- **Analyzing your email pattern:** Some add-ons come with analytics capabilities. Most of them will be of little use for you on a daily basis, but you can still try to use them to your benefit. Knowing the people you exchange email with most frequently, as well as corresponding response times, can help you gauge your level of interaction with key people. Be sure to keep your boss (i.e., the person who is in charge of your promotions) in your "Top 5" of most frequent contacts, and try to maintain reasonably short response times for his or her messages.

IF YOUR COMPANY PROHIBITS INSTALLING SOFTWARE

I know that some corporate policies rule out installing unapproved software. Apart from the core applications, there is usually not much you will be relying on every day anyway. Therefore, I don't expect most corporate IT groups to even have these add-ons on their radar. This being said, installation is likely not permitted. In that case, use common sense.

What are all the options you could use to get approval? Speak to other colleagues first to see if they have already installed some similar solution. Alternatively, catch up with the folks in your IT department. Approach this topic casually, and avoid written communication on the matter. They will not be very welcoming to the idea of using unapproved software—especially when such questions generate a permanent email trail. Perhaps they are using it too, even if it is not included in the "recommended software catalogue." If you do not ask, you'll never know. For more information on how to best deal with your IT department, see Chapter 11.

If this fails, consider installing the add-on anyway. Ask for forgiveness in case someone finds fault with your approach later on.[14] Remember, at times, it is easier to beg forgiveness than ask permission.

Managing Email With Your Email Client

Even the most sophisticated Outlook settings do not guarantee that you will be able to manage the massive amount of email flooding in from Day 1. Therefore, you will want to consider improving your own email management skills.

This section covers the most important tips you should consider adopting right away. In essence, this serves as a brief introduction to daily email management techniques that can be learned and applied instantly. It is not a precise science but rather a matter of awareness that should be followed by the willingness to proceed accordingly.

Shortcuts

There are countless keyboard shortcuts available. Do some further research in case you feel that something is missing or just to find out what else you might adopt. For the time being, I strongly suggest getting comfortable using the following shortcuts. They will help you navigate around your inbox faster and don't require an engineering degree to understand:

- Ctrl+R: Reply to email
- Alt+R: Reply to all in email
- Alt+W: Forward email
- Ctrl+M, or F9: Send/Receive all
- Alt+S: Send email

Templates

One of the easiest ways to save time managing email is to use templates. Templates can be used for all types of recurring email communication. Meeting or telephone conference invitations as well as newsletters or responses to recurring customer requests fall into this category.

However, don't spend time searching for official Outlook templates. You need scripts tailored to your particular situation and personal style. Save some of the best content that is sent to you in your initial weeks on the job, and then try to leverage as much as possible while establishing your own style.

Throughout this book, you will find sample scripts based on the case scenario. You can find free, ready-to-use templates at GotTheJobNowWhat.com/Bonus.

FLAGGING

In Outlook, you can flag emails, indicating when/if you have to get back to an item or act on it. There is actually some methodology behind the flagging process, but it is not very useful in practice. Thus, just mark everything with a flag and then work your way down.

What you might want to do is scan all incoming emails and immediately decide how to handle them. Delete? Archive? Immediately respond? Come back at a later point? Deleting and archiving are self-explanatory. You simply hit the right buttons or use drag-and-drop to get the job done. An immediate response should only be considered if the task takes less than two minutes and the matter is urgent and important (for internal requests) or simply urgent (for customer requests). If none of these cases apply, set a flag and get back to it later.

For all other cases (i.e., incoming email you need to follow up on), you will set a flag right next to it. Try to keep your inbox as clean as possible. Ideally, there will be flags on each line. Get back to it when you have the free time or whenever you typically clear up your inbox. You can learn more about how to manage your to-do lists in Chapter 9.

Rules

There are many rules you can set up to handle incoming email, but none of them are truly required. If you only consider three rules, they should be the following:

- **Delay Outgoing Emails by 1 Minute:** There is only one rule that you immediately want to include: the one-minute delay rule for outgoing email. This is mission-critical and might save your career at some point. You will run into all sorts of issues on a daily basis: missing or sending the wrong attachments, an incomplete list of recipients, incorrect text in the email body, or simply mistaking a customer for an internal email recipient. The potential problems are tremendous, and you will be glad that you had access to pull back an email after hitting the "send" button. One minute is usually enough for your subconscious to kick in. Search online for "Outlook 1-minute delay" and follow the steps provided.

  With this in place, any outgoing email will be kept in your outbox for one minute before actually being transferred. Share this point with your colleagues. They will thank you one day. Why shouldn't you go for an extra two or three minutes? Because of time. You don't have any to spare, especially when your boss wants some file urgently. The one-minute rule should be kept in any event. Do not play around with it. Stick to the system, even if your boss does not agree. This may be your first opportunity to push back.

- **Schedule Emails to Be Sent at a Future Date:** At times, you have some bandwidth and you think of ways to cross off a few minor items on your to-do list. Following up on a summer event that your boss has asked you to help organize? This is the perfect time to get that task out of the way. However, you do not want to do this immediately, not only because it is not critical (as external client work is) but also because you run the risk of receiving an immediate response by email or phone. This isn't necessarily a problem, but chances are that it may kill your day. Don't let that happen.

Instead, schedule your follow-up email for some later hour in the day, if not on a different day altogether (Friday afternoons come to mind). This will help you cross off items on your list while making sure that nothing of minor importance interferes with your working day.

- **Send Email Straight From of the Subject Line:** You can further increase your efficiency by firing off email straight from the subject line. To do this, you could create a rule that automatically sends your email once you have hit, for example, the space key five times in a row. Ideally, you should combine this with the one-minute delay rule by creating an exception, namely one that says, "subject contains..." and five consecutive spaces.

There is one more recommendation of what *not* to do when it comes to Outlook rules. Some people swear by automatically moving all email they have been Cc'd on into a designated "CC Folder". Unless you are already drowning in work, I do not see any justification for a junior resource to apply such rule. When you start, you not only have to be on top of everything that you are somewhat involved in (even something as minor as a Cc in an email), but you can also learn from most incoming communication.

General Thoughts on Writing Email

Now that we know how to treat email from within Outlook, let's take a look at actually composing emails in a business environment. This will not be the easiest part, even if it might not appear worthy of discussion. I hope this section will make you think differently because when email is used inappropriately, you will easily come off as unprofessional.[15]

When to Write and When Not to Write

Email is free. Or is it? Research shows that the average businessperson spends anywhere between 28–35 percent of his or her workday on managing email.[16] If one-third of your day is spent on email communication,[17] we can definitely put a price tag on it. Therefore, think twice before sending email.

- Is the email necessary or could you achieve the same result over the phone, via corporate messenger (chat), or in person?

- Is the content of the email contentious, containing material that should therefore not be stored electronically?

- Is this a topic that should be informally discussed first?

What this boils down to is that you should not send email when the same objective could be accomplished by speaking to the recipient in person or on the phone. You also want to limit email to those occasions where trust has been established and the topic at hand is uncontentious.

Whom to Write

Obviously, you want to limit the number of recipients of any email. Recipients should have some type of stake in the communication you send. "Stake" means that they will be affected by an outcome of your email or will have to follow up on specific tasks drawn from it.

There is one caveat to this discussion. When sending out emails to external clients, do not assume that your manager is too busy and should not be copied in on the email. If you have considered carefully whether your message qualifies as email at all, then don't second-guess whether your senior should be included in the recipient list. He or she has to be included, unless instructed otherwise.

Particularly when starting out, juniors often exclude senior people in an attempt to save them from email burden. However, you can be sure that one email will simply not cut it. In fact, this approach backfires for most juniors. You will have to establish trust first. From Day 1, despite having been hired, trust still has to be earned. And that takes time. Therefore, include your boss or immediate superior at all times, unless you are asked not to.

Also, remember that some people take the sequence of recipients very seriously. Carefully consider whom to include in what order. The general rule is that external recipients come before internal ones, while senior recipients come before more junior ones.

THE POWER OF CC

With a minimal direct recipient list in your email, you can be more liberal in terms of whom you carbon copy into your email (Cc'ing). As a junior, you will want to get your name out there, and rather than running down the hallway naked, you want to do this with business topics. Copy everyone that you can think of as somewhat relevant to the content. Err on the side of adding more, and wait until you are told not to Cc someone.

For email that you want to have on hand quickly in which you need to ensure everything has been delivered correctly, Cc yourself too. You will hit send, and after a minute (provided you have enabled the one-minute delay), you will receive the very same email.

Drag and drop this email into the folder where it belongs. This will help you keep all the important pieces together. Otherwise, you will eventually have to dig out this email from the "Sent" folder.

The Curse of "Reply All" – It Doesn't Exist

Contrary to what you may read online, the "Reply All" button is going to be your best friend. In fact, for juniors, this should be the default when responding to incoming email. Usually, you will be at the receiving end of an email requesting some type of action. Recipients of that original email should also be kept in the loop when you are ready to respond. This includes a simple confirmation that you have understood the request made (which you will have to send) as well as any final deliverable.

If you do drop people from the list of recipients, they may start to wonder and eventually question your reliability. This might sound harsh, but the world of business is characterized by a culture of drive and achievement. Therefore, it does not lend itself to niceties for the pure sake of them. People treat each other respectfully but can be just as quick to find shortcomings in others.

When to Use Bcc

Bcc (blind carbon copy) is rarely used, and for good reason. As a general rule, anyone you include in email communication should be visible to all other recipients, but there are exceptions.

For example, imagine that you are reprimanding a team member (unlikely in your early years). You should ensure that your team leader is in the loop, but that might not necessarily require him to be entered in the "To:" or "Cc:" fields. Such action would likely create more tension between you and the person you sought to coach or constructively critique.

Another example may be Bcc'ing your mentor in an email to your manager where you are raising important concerns about your own role on the team (e.g., when understaffed). You probably would not want to highlight to your manager that you are involving other people in the organization, especially if they are senior to him or her. However, keep in mind, should your mentor hit "Reply All," the response will go to all people on the original distribution. Therefore, refrain from using Bcc unless you have a very good reason to.

WRITING EFFECTIVE EMAIL

Before looking at a specific example of how to write an email, we will discuss the most important components that you should consider, namely the subject line, the email body, and attachments.

THE SUBJECT LINE

The subject line serves as the headline of your email. Make it stand out through clarity. Try to be as specific and concise as possible. An ideal subject line is characterized by the following.

- **Brevity:** Limit your subject line to between five to eight words unless it is necessary to go beyond that. This will ensure that your subject line can be read on most mobile devices without cutting off halfway.

- **Standard convention:** People like consistency, and the more reliably you can provide that, the better it will be for you and your standing in the company (unless you screw up in your actual work). Also, make sure to utilize commonly used abbreviations (if any).

- **Clear task:** You can add tremendous value to recipients if you help them decide what they are supposed to do. Do not require them to actually read your email to understand that. If something is for informational purposes only, mention this in the subject line.

There are two possible objectives to achieve with your subject line in a business context. The choice between the two will depend on your situation. Common sense and some learning through experience will be your guides. These two objectives are listed below.

1. Inform the recipient about the content of your email: This is likely the most common mailing sent by juniors. Examples include progress updates or the submission of deliverables. Be specific and allow the recipient to understand what your email is about, such as "Project X Proposal – Storyboard DRAFT." This email should enclose a draft storyboard, or structure, of the proposal for Project X.

2. Make a call to action: This depends on the content of your email and the particular recipient. I've provided examples I have effectively used in the past:

    –   REVIEW: Asking the recipient to review either the mailing itself or an attachment and to provide feedback (e.g., a draft presentation)

    –   REQUEST: Indicating that a request is being made through this message (e.g., approval of vacation or training)

    –   FYI (For Your Information): Informative content, which should be read but not (immediately) acted upon (e.g., market trend reports of which the team should be aware)

    –   CONFIDENTIAL: Highlighting any piece of information that should not be shared beyond a close group of colleagues (e.g., sharing initial thoughts on organizational restructuring)

- URGENT: Calling for immediate attention (e.g., asking for ad hoc support or critical information)

- LOW PRIO: Indicating a non-urgent and only partly relevant email message (e.g., useful information for future marketing activities)

You might wonder why one could not simply use the flagging function in Outlook to indicate the level of importance before sending an email. The answer? Many people already do this. Most emails tend to be of "High Importance." This is so common that, based on my experience, most recipients have stopped using those flags as a guideline for importance. In fact, I have found that "Low Importance" emails trigger a much better response.

THE EMAIL BODY

What was said about subject lines also holds true for the email body. Brevity and clarity are essential. When composing your email, always ask yourself the following questions:

1. Is what I am writing clear? If not, rewrite it. Minimize the amount of email ping-pong by carefully composing crystal-clear messages up front.

2. Is something redundant? If so, delete it. If the message could do without it, then there is no reason to include it.

3. Am I being clear about my expectations of the reader? Is this an informational email or am I asking the reader to do something? Review and specify whatever could be misunderstood.

After drafting the email, you should once again confirm that brevity and courtesy are balanced. When dealing with senior colleagues or customers, seeking brevity does not mean that you can cut short on formalities, such as proper form of address and correct spelling.

In addition, you want to be very explicit about the intention of your email and the request for the recipient. If the recipient is to act, mention this explicitly. It is good practice to mention your expectation in the first paragraph of your mailing, as demonstrated below:

"I am sending you the latest XYZ document for your review."

Furthermore, state the deadline for when the feedback needs to be incorporated. Mention this even in the rare event that no deadline exists. This will not only allow you to schedule a follow up, but recipients will also be able to accurately register the request and get back to you in time. A commonly used phrase in closing your mailing could read:

"Your review and feedback by Friday, October 10th, (COB/ Close of Business) will be much appreciated."

Notice that I have highlighted some parts in bold (not underlined or italics). This is a good practice to denote key information.

One final remark: For very important email messages, ask one of your trusted colleagues to briefly review the email prior to sending. This so-called Four-Eyes Principle can help identify wrong information, missing parts, or any other aspects that could weaken your email.

ATTACHMENTS

Now, let's turn our attention to email attachments. There are at least five aspects of which to be aware. Don't skip this section unless you want to be on the receiving end of an angry manager call.

- **Mind the maximum size of attachments:** Most corporate networks limit not only the size of email inboxes, but also the size of attachments.[18] If you need to exchange large files (i.e., when handing over a USB key will not be an option)[19], try to use the corporate messenger tool, your firm's shared drive, or other cloud-sharing solutions. For the latter, discuss this with your manager beforehand to avoid any legal implications.

- **Consider the compatibility of file types:** Usually, you do not have to be concerned about what file types you are sending out. Microsoft Office is widely used. However, there is one exception—senior leadership. Leaders are increasingly using iPads to manage their day-to-day operations. "So what?" you may wonder. Try to send that "Project Steering Committee" PowerPoint presentation to them. Chances are that they will not be able to read it properly. Formatting might be all over the place. Don't let that happen. Instead, when sending files to senior leaders, think ahead and provide the file as both a PowerPoint and a PDF, and mention that you added the same file in two different formats deliberately:

  "For your convenience, I have attached the presentation both as a PPT and a PDF. I hope this will be useful to you."

  This will serve two purposes. It will show you had the recipient's needs in mind, and it will prevent someone from having to ask why you attached the same file twice.

- **Limit the number of attachments:** Do not send more attachments than necessary. If there are other relevant files, mention them and offer to provide them upon request or make them available in a shared environment via a link.

- **Use standard file-naming conventions for attachments:** Never send files with cryptic file names. Recipients should not struggle to make sense of your attachments. The exact naming convention may differ if you are working on different project teams and depends on your personal style. Seek guidance from your manager on this. For your own purposes, ensure file names:

- Are ordered chronologically
- Are not overly extensive in length
- Do not include special characters (e.g., ~ ! @ # $ % ^ & * ( ) ` ; < > ? , [ ] { } ' ")
- Avoid spaces (hint: use underscores or dashes)
- Include version numbers (if applicable)

In Project Insight, the project run with GTL, a good and bad example may look as follows:

- Insight Project Plan for GTL-23 September 2016.ppt (bad)
- 20160923_GTL_Insight_Project Plan_v01.ppt (good, as it guarantees the documents are date-sorted, no matter what platform they eventually land on)
- GTL_Insight_Project Plan_20160923_v01.ppt (good alternative)

- **Mention attachments in the email body:** When you attach files to your email, be explicit about them in the actual email, particularly when sending more than one file. The following two rules have worked well for others in the past.

Mention your files in the full text but also separate them out as lists. You should introduce your attachments starting with:

"Please find attached ..."

Mention file types in your attachment description as "PPT," "XLS," "DOC," or "PDF." The full file name is only required if you send several files of the same file type (i.e., provide file names if you sent two PowerPoint files but not if you sent one Excel and one PowerPoint file).

GOOD VS. BAD EMAIL: AN EXAMPLE

We have discussed the pitfalls of writing business emails. Let us now compare what good and bad emails actually look like side by side.

As part of Project Insight, Mark has helped to develop a presentation and some spreadsheets for the project's steering committee meeting. All those involved in the project, as well as FT and GTL leadership are invited to attend. Manuela Perez (project lead) has asked Mark to send the information to Peter Jackson (FT CEO) ahead of time. The presentation includes some initial findings and recommendations based on an analysis conducted by Manuela and Mark (and support from GTL's Andrew Seagull).

First, we look at a poor email that Mark might write (Table 4). This showcases what some may assume to be right. Afterward, I will illustrate what Mark writes instead (Table 5).

Area	Example	Comment
To:	P Jackson	
Cc:	-	Where is Manuela, the project manager? You always need to ensure your project manager/senior is in the loop.
Subject line	Fwd: Re: Draft Deck	This email can be about anything, and a senior person juggling different topics will have a hard time figuring this out from the subject line.
Body	Hi,	Regardless of how much time you have, you should stick to certain formalities. Mentioning somebody's name is a must.
	In preparation of tomorrow's Steering Committee meeting, please find attached the draft presentation.	Peter Jackson could have a hard time figuring out what project is concerned.
	More specifically, you will find: • PPT: Steering Committee presentation (DRAFT) • XLS: 2 data sets used for the presentation	Two XLS data sets have been enclosed. For clarity purposes, they should be singled out here as well.
	In case you have any questions or remarks, please do not hesitate to get back to us anytime.	Clearly, a C-level executive can come back with change requests anytime. But it helps to indicate by what time you will need to incorporate feedback.
	Best, Mark	
Attach-ment	Steering Comm_09 14_v02.ppt	The PPT is missing a specific date; it is unclear what the date refers to. Mark is also missing a PDF version.
	20160902_Insight_Dataset_v05.xls 20160905_Insight_Other Analysis_v02.xls	The purpose of the two XLS attachments is not explained. Also, are they the right versions given that they appear to be from early September?

Table 4: Poor Email Example

Area	Example	Comment
To:	P Jackson	
Cc:	M Perez, M Johnson	The project manager should be cc'd, and Mark might want to consider including himself too.
Subject line	GTL – Insight – STC Mtg – Deck DRAFT	This subject line is extensive, covering everything the senior exec needs to understand what it is about.
		Peter Jackson understands that this is about Project Insight with GTL and that the presentation (i.e., deck) is a draft.
		Note: Steering Committee is commonly abbreviated as STC.
Body	Dear Peter,	Mentioned name ✓
	In preparation of tomorrow's Steering Committee meeting with GTL, please find attached the draft presentation.	This is great; we know exactly what this email is about – a steering committee at GTL taking place tomorrow.
	More specifically, you will find:	This makes it very clear: there are three files for Peter to consider.
	• PPT: Steering Committee presentation (DRAFT)	
	• PDF: Steering Committee presentation (DRAFT)	
	• XLS: Dataset used for the presentation	
	For your convenience, I have attached the presentation both as PPT and PDF.	Peter understands why the draft has been attached twice.
	In case you have any questions or remarks, please do not hesitate to get back to us anytime.	
	We plan on finalizing the document by tomorrow, **September 14, 2016, 10 a.m.,** to allow all participants to review up front.	Here, we make it clear by when we would need feedback from Peter in order to ensure that we can deliver the material to all attendees ahead of time.
	Best, Mark	
Attach-ment	20160913_GTL_Insight_Steering Comm_09 14_v02.ppt	All files are easily recognizable. We know what they are about – complete with date, client, project, topic, and version number.
	20160913_GTL_Insight_Steering Comm_09 14_v02.pdf	
	20160913_GTL_Insight_Dataset_v05.xls	

Table 5: Good Email Example

KEY TAKEAWAYS

- Set your email client up for success. Enhance your email management capabilities by making efficiency-boosting adjustments to the settings and using third-party add-ons.

- Be efficient. Adopt email management techniques that help you get the job done faster. Shortcuts, templates, rules, etc., should become part of your standard repertoire.

- Reply to everything. This can be overwhelming at first, but you have to react to incoming email quickly. Whether asking for clarification or confirming your understanding, take action.

- Reply to all. When you are the recipient, make sure that everyone receives your response. Hitting "Reply All" should be your default option.

- Don't leave room for interpretation. Communicate clearly. All major email components—subject line, email body, attachments—should aid the recipients' understanding.

[7]

Mastering Phone Communication

"Not returning phone calls is the severest
form of torture in the civilized world."

Marisha Pessl, *Special Topics in Calamity Physics*

ONE OF THE FIRST things I learned on the job was how to set up telephone conferences. In fact, this was the very first task I was given. Unfortunately, there were some minor hiccups I would have liked to avoid. In order to save you from experiencing the same, this chapter highlights the most important points regarding phone communication. Keep in mind, this is not a guide on how to conduct sales calls.

First, I will give you my general take on phone communication in business. This includes some best practices for making calls in a professional work environment. We will then turn our attention to an often-used medium: telephone conferences. Here, we will look at common pitfalls and discuss how to effectively set up telephone conferences. Afterward, I will illustrate what to do, and especially what not to do, when being either host or participant to telephone conferences.

THE BASICS OF USING A PHONE

Let us start by discussing something so obvious that it should not require any deeper explanation: calling other people. In our day and age, many people feel more comfortable using instant messengers than the phone. This can become a problem, as calling someone is the best way to go in most work environments. Solving issues by phone tends to be quicker and less prone to incorrect interpretation than email, and definitely beats instant messaging for more complex topics. However, remember that personal interaction is still far superior. Thus, walking down one floor and speaking in person should be considered the best option if possible.

GETTING TO KNOW YOUR TOOLS

Before you actually make the first call, you should familiarize yourself with the phone system used in your office. You will want to develop an understanding of its basic functionality. Most likely, you will be able to retrieve the official manual from the manufacturer's website. Download it and skim through the table of contents. If you have never worked in an office environment before, you will be amazed by what you can do with modern telephones.

Given that each machine is different, no further details on navigating your phone system can be provided here. Nevertheless, try to figure out how you would accomplish the following:

- Invite a third party to an ongoing call

- Connect different parties with each other

- Forward calls

- Enter digits when prompted to do so (e.g., when you want to join telephone conferences and need to enter a code; depending on the model, you might need to press an additional button like the "shift" key on your computer)

Having pointed out the basics, let's look at the actual conversational part.

Making Calls

Before you call anyone, colleagues and external parties alike, write down the key points you would like to discuss. Make it a habit to prepare this not only in your head but also on paper. This will ensure that you do not lose track of your point while making the call.

Have you ever received a call from someone that included something along the lines of, "Let's see.... There was something else...." What impression has that made on you? Probably not a very good one. Prepare for conversations up front and be seen as professional. Similarly, you want to come up with a standard opener. Never get caught searching for the right words. Come up with them once, embed them in your memory, and then focus on getting material things done. Clearly, this opener depends on your personality, but make sure it is somewhat upbeat.

Every so often, you will end up leaving a voice mail message. For some, this might be new information, but the "beep" is prompting you to leave a message. Far too often, people just end the call upon realizing that no one was going to pick up anyhow. Don't make that mistake. If you spend time calling to begin with, take the extra minute to leave a message.

Leaving voice mail messages is similar to the opener discussed before. It should be a standard message that you develop once, commit to memory, and then adjust only slightly depending on the list of points that you prepared to discuss. For example, in Project Insight,

Mark might try to follow up with GTL's Operations Analyst Andrew Seagull regarding some operational figures he received earlier:

> *Hi, this is Mark (optional: of Future Technologies),*
>
> *It's Tuesday, September 6th, just after 2 p.m.*
>
> *I was calling to confirm my understanding of the figures of the UK warehouses you sent me earlier and to clarify specifically why the figures for the Bristol site only cover 2014.*
>
> *Please call me back when you are free at 001-123-445-445. Thanks, bye.*

Having set the ground rules for phone communication in a business environment, let us now turn to telephone conferences.

THE TROUBLE WITH TELEPHONE CONFERENCES

Telephone conferences are very common in business. In fact, they have become so pervasive that some key people in organizations have entire days blocked out for telephone conferences—often back to back and at times simultaneously.

The purpose of telephone conferences is very similar to ordinary meetings, namely, ensuring alignment among a group of people, generating buy-in, providing updates, and deciding on potential next steps.

Unfortunately, many people do not treat meetings and telephone conferences the same way. If you are meant to be in a meeting room at 3 p.m., you will probably be there on time, just like everyone else. However, for telephone conferences, it's a whole different world. Hosts are late, attendees are late, confirmed attendees do not dial in—you name it. Let me share how you can do better and excel where many others frequently fail.

How to Set Up Telephone Conferences

It was my second day at work when my manager asked me to schedule an update call with my fellow colleagues. Maybe it was just me, but in the heat of the moment, I simply went ahead and tried to schedule the call only to realize that I lacked any real details.

First, I was not given a list of points to include when sending out the invitation. Thus, I had to go back to my manager and ask for information after I had already agreed to send the invitation, which is never a good thing. From this experience, I learned that it is good practice to create a list of questions and have them answered all at once. For telephone conferences, it is important to cover the below points:

- **Discussion topics:** Clarify with your manager what the key discussion points of the call will be. If you can make suggestions, great. Otherwise, let your manager guide you.

- **Time and date:** A telephone conference should ideally be scheduled as soon as the idea is raised. With busy schedules, that will be a challenge. Confirm with your manager if there is a deadline for when the call needs to take place. Knowing this is crucial to lock in time slots when working with senior leaders' assistants.

- **Duration:** What is the minimum period of time required? Think in fifteen-minute increments here. Just because most email clients suggest full-hour or half-hour invitations does not mean that you should stick to them. If the objective of the telephone conference can be achieved within a few minutes, then do yourself and the attendees a favor by being brief. Clarify with your manager what to aim for.

- **Attendees:** Are there any key people that have to be on the call? Will some of them require you to check with their assistants beforehand? For example, many senior executives have someone taking care of their administrative tasks and thus do not expect you to directly bother them with meeting requests.

- **Location of attendees and corresponding dial-in numbers:** Keep in mind that your local dial-in code is of little use to those calling in from other countries. Unless there is a good reason not to (and the only valid one would be that you have no international dial-in codes), carefully consider where attendees will call from and provide them with corresponding dial-in codes. Do not simply paste a list of numbers into the email body or, worse, attach a PDF document or insert a link to some website. Provide all codes that might be used both in the email body and in the meeting location field.

- **Clarification of which passcode and chair code to use:** Someone will be the host of the call. When you are just starting out, you probably will not have personal dial-in codes for yourself yet. Thus, the chair code for the host and dial-in codes for the attendees are likely to be provided by your manager.

In the rare event of you being asked to set up a meeting series, leverage the full power of your email client and set this up with a single invite. People like accepting invites once. People do not like accepting invites to the same meeting on different dates twelve times.

For example, at the start of Project Insight, Mark has been asked to schedule a weekly thirty-minute update call between the FT and GTL (Table 6).

The key here is to be very specific and think from the recipient's perspective. Make it crystal clear what is expected and make joining the call as easy as possible. You could use this example as a template for your own "telco invites." An electronic version is available for free at GotTheJobNowWhat.com/bonus.

When you are setting up a telephone conference, you will inevitably run into difficulties. Some people will not be available, while others will simply not respond. Keep track of your progress and proactively provide feedback to your manager. This will allow you to cover yourself and potentially let your manager jump in if necessary.

Let's now go deeper into two different telephone conference scenarios. First, I will describe what it means to be a good participant in a conference call. Afterward, I will explain what you should do when you are hosting a telephone conference.

Area	Example	Comment
To:	J Cazeneuve (Project Sponsor GTL) R Grant (Project Lead GTL) M Gray (Head of Birmingham GTL) A Seagull (Operations Analyst GTL) M Perez (Project Lead FT)	All those required belong to the "To:" section. Mark also needs to do this in the appropriate order, i.e., external client staff from senior to junior, internal staff from senior to junior.
Cc:	B Cho (CEO GTL) P Jackson (CEO FT)	Optional attendees can be cc'd. It is not common for executives to dial in to every weekly update call. Sometimes, however, they wish to be kept in the loop – just like B Cho and P Jackson.
Subject line	Project Insight: Weekly Update Call	The subject line should be short and relevant. The purpose of the call should be clear from the subject line. Here, Mark mentions the project, and topic.
Location	Telco – UK +44 123 456 789; US +1 123 456 789; PIN 123456#	Include all relevant information, and enable attendees to dial-in directly from the location line, as this will be right in their calendars, too. (Note: The PIN is the participant passcode.)

Body	Dear all,	This email body assumes Mark has done his homework. Thus, the majority of people should be able to accept.
	Hereby I am scheduling a brief 30-min. call about Project Insight.	
	Please find dial-in details below.	You don't want to clutter up your invitation with dial-in details upfront. Save this till the end.
	The objective of the call is to:	You want to be as specific as possible. If there are certain documents to be reviewed or discussed, mention this here, too.
	• Summarize key accomplishments	
	• Discuss next steps	
	• AOB (any other business)	
	Dial-in details:	Provide dial-in details, i.e., international dial-in numbers and the participant passcode.
	UK: +44 123 456 789	
	US: +1 123 456 789	
	Participant passcode: 123456#	Include the chair code directly, or mention who will be the host.
	Chair code: Mark / 555555#	
	In case this time does not suit you, please let me know (by providing two alternative time slots).	You want to require people to reach out to you in case they cannot join.
	Thanks,	Depending on your style or standing, you may request alternative time slots be provided when declining the invite.
	Mark	
	Contact Details	Adding your signature is key. Make it easy for people to contact you directly from the invite. This includes at a minimum your cell phone number and email address.
	Mark Johnson	
	Mobile: +1 123 445 445	
	Email: m.johnson@futuretech.com	

Table 6: Telephone Conference Invitation

How to Be a Good Telco Participant

For starters, you will not be expected to have much input in telephone conferences early in your career. Unless you have some expert knowledge (e.g., access to key data), the sole reason for you to dial in to the call is to take notes and learn.

So what do you actually do in a call when you are not expected to talk? Keep a low profile. Remain silent unless you are prompted to speak, and do not screw up. You could ask stupid questions (trust me, they exist) or be in a noisy place and fail to press your mute button.

Don't! If you do, your manager will reprimand you, and you may not get invited to future calls. Instead, do what common sense suggests:

- **Dial in early:** Regardless of your schedule, as a junior resource, you will have no reason to dial in late. It is simply not acceptable. If you really cannot make it in time, let the host know in advance.

- **State your name (and potentially your office and role):** When you dial in, you are supposed to make people aware that you have joined the call. Be brief. Stating your name is usually sufficient. In case you are a complete newbie to the group of attendees, you can add which office you are from or what role you are fulfilling. In our example case, this may be:

  Hi, this is Mark Johnson dialing in from the Boston office.

  or:

  Hi, this is Mark Johnson, from the Finance department.

- **Be online:** Unless traveling is part of your work, you should have access to your computer most of the time. Therefore, by all means, fire up your corporate messaging tool (e.g., Skype for Business). Be online. Consider opening chat windows with the telco host (unless you are sitting next to him) and other attendees who you might want to communicate with if necessary.

- **Shut up and listen:** No questions. No remarks. Dial in, state your name, and, unless requested to speak up, say good-bye when closing the call. If you have some crucial point to raise, check with your manager or closest colleague first; but do this on mute or by using instant messengers, text messages, or email. Do not try to impress (yet).

- **Be attentive—but remain quiet:** So what are those occasions where you have to reach out to contact attendees via a messaging app? Emergencies, and there are many. Someone might be having trouble getting a point across, and you might be able to come to the rescue because you have that exact project plan right in front of you. Some figures might be discussed and further thought through, and you can quickly fire up your spreadsheet and run through those numbers. Don't jump in and provide those preliminary results though. Forward the information to the host or your manager and let him or her decide how to proceed with the information.

  It is also worth noting that you should not attempt to multitask. Do not play with your phone or text friends while on the call. It is a bad habit, despite the fact that some managers may also do it.

- **Take notes:** You might not be asked to write anything down, but you will eventually be asked to prepare a draft write-up of the main discussion points and decisions. Even if it is an informal call, your manager might casually ask you how you understood a certain discussion point. It is better to say that you will look through your notes and realize that you have nothing important to add than not to have anything to review to begin with.

In short, as a junior, you will be considered a good participant if you do not screw up and are able to support in the background.

How to Be a Good Telco Host

At the beginning of your career, you will rarely be asked to host a call in a project-related context. In such cases, you might only be required to set up the telephone conference and open it at the appropriate time. Your manager will likely be by your side and act as the host. Nevertheless, for some internal work, you will occasionally be required to host a call. The key here is to not take this lightly but to instead consider this as a realistic learning opportunity. People are forgiving, especially with respect to juniors. Everyone started out at some point, so people know what it's like.

Having said this, you will be remembered in a bad light if you do not meet the minimum expectations. Therefore, it is absolutely crucial to focus on a few key factors that will set you up for a solid performance.

- **Dial in early:** Open the call at least five minutes prior to the official starting time. You do not want to realize that the line doesn't work when everyone else is already desperately trying to dial in or worse...waiting for the host. Treat a telephone conference just like you would any other meeting and arrange yourself accordingly.

- **Start the call on time:** Once you have opened the call, people will be dialing in more or less on time (*read*: they rarely do). Depending on the situation, you might be required to fill some time. Use common sense here. Based on experience in past calls, there is a good chance that senior people will happily jump in and start brief conversations with each other on various (related) topics. In any event, never wait for more than five minutes before kicking off. Unless key people confirmed that they would be dialing in late (e.g., because they are landing at an airport) and requested that the group wait, go ahead.

- **Confirm attendance as you go:** [Beep!] "Now joining..." People usually do not dial in at the same time. Taking our case scenario as an example, telco host Mark should jump in right away by asking:

  Hi, this is Mark. Who has just joined?

  This is a crucial aspect of hosting. Many people do not immediately state their names. Write down each name or check the person off on your list of attendees. Depending on the size of the group, briefly state who else has already dialed in. This gets you talking and establishes you as the host, despite potentially being the most junior member on the call.

- **Briefly sum up attendance when officially kicking off:** Once you are ready to begin, repeat the names of all the attendees once again. This allows everyone to be on the same page.

- **Repeat the objectives of the call:** Even though you will have already covered key discussion points in your invite to the call, don't expect everyone to have read it. Most people are either too busy or lazy to do it. Thus, quickly summarize what will be discussed and then get moving!

- **Let them talk:** You are the host of the call, which means that you're in charge, but just like when throwing a party at your place, you're not expected to participate in every discussion. Manage the meeting, but don't try to dominate it. Let the big guys get on with it, but be sure to keep an eye on your watch and keep the team on track.

- **End on time:** Always. Watch. The. Time. This is key! Try to finish early, if possible, and never end late. If there is a push to extend the call from some participants, make that desire public by asking the group if that is acceptable for each and every person on the call. Otherwise, you will be held accountable for making someone late for a succeeding meeting.

- **Summarize key decision points:** Before finishing the call, thank everyone for their participation, summarize key takeaways, and highlight the next steps.

- **Send out minutes or a brief write-up:** The majority of calls will require some sort of follow up. Otherwise, what was the point of having the telephone conference to begin with? Depending on the requirements, a short write-up should be shared with the attendees within twenty-four hours of the call. Detailed guidance on how to write effective meeting minutes can be found in the bonus material at GotTheJobNowWhat.com/bonus.

In the rare event that you have to share your screen during the call, think carefully about what other people should be able to see. Ideally, use a second screen that you use for sharing material. Alternatively (and absolutely critical if you do not have a second screen available), share only specific programs (e.g., Microsoft PowerPoint or Excel). You want to avoid other people viewing your inbox, notifications, or, worst of all, messenger windows from other people on the call. If there is one underrated career-limiting move, it is this: sharing information and content with people who were not supposed to have access to it.

In short, hosting a telephone conference is not rocket science. With some preparation (and practice), you will be able to smoothly navigate through all sorts of calls, some of which might be heated debates. As long as you are doing your homework and closely following the guidelines above, the potential pitfalls will be minimal.

Key Takeaways

♦ Learn how to use the phone. Whenever starting at a new workplace, familiarize yourself with the functionality of the phone. At the very least, understand how to connect, merge, and forward calls.

♦ Prepare for every call. Always have a clear idea of what your objective and discussion points in a call will be. Use standard scripts for both the opener and voice mail messages to simplify your communication.

♦ Don't reinvent telephone conference invitations. Use standard templates to save time and ensure that critical information is captured.

♦ Don't screw up when you participate in telcos. As a junior employee, keep a low profile, listen attentively, and avoid hiccups (e.g., being surrounded by noise and not being on mute).

♦ You have to be capable of running the show. While it is more common to be asked to take notes, career starters can be expected to be able to host telephone conferences. Learn from every call you attend by taking actual notes, even when not instructed to do so, and take charge when requested.

[8]

On Meetings

"The least productive people are usually the ones who are most in favor of holding meetings."

Thomas Sowell

I F YOUR WORKING REALITY is anything like the case in most industries, one thing is guaranteed: there will be plenty of meetings. While it is in our best interest to minimize the number of meetings, this is a discussion someone else besides you should have. Do not waste your time reading about strategies for how to convince your boss of skipping meetings. Unless you can deliver significant value while absent, do not bother with such a strategy. It will likely backfire.

To help you execute properly from Day 1, we will first look at the requirements and key tasks for a junior-level resource that is helping to organize a meeting. Because this is what you will probably be involved in from the very beginning. We will break this section down into three phases: before, during, and after the meeting.

We will adopt the same approach as when you are invited to a meeting as a participant. We will conclude the chapter with an overview of meeting invitations, how to write them, and what to do when you are on the receiving end. If you are looking for detailed information about how to hold meetings yourself, refer to the Appendix for additional resources, as this is not included in this guide.

Helping to Organize Meetings

One of the first things people usually ask juniors to help with is meeting preparation. Unless you have extensive knowledge in an area important to the meeting, your role will be to support the meeting organizer. Don't take this lightly. Try to anticipate what could go wrong and take precautionary measures.

Let's look at the most important things that should be considered based on input from several seasoned industry veterans. They have certain expectations of juniors. If you fulfill these expectations, then you will have a successful start with your manager. Don't feel too proud to support on certain tasks. No matter how mundane the task may seem, take it, embrace it, and make the life of your manager easier. Your effort will be recognized.

Before the Meeting

Your support to the meeting host will primarily take place before the actual meeting. Your initial tasks might be of low importance to you, but they are still crucial to ensure a smooth delivery of the actual event. Make no mistake, regardless of how small, irrelevant, or below your qualifications certain requests may appear to be, consider this the price you must pay to earn your manager's trust.

Some typical tasks in this phase are finding suitable time slots with secretaries, sourcing and collating material, and booking rooms. When preparing a meeting, keep in mind the following:

- **Agree on meeting output:** You should have a clear idea of what the expected output and corresponding requirements will be. In case of a more informal briefing, there might not be any tangible output. At other times, multiple topics may be discussed, decisions made, and tasks assigned. In such cases, the essence of the meeting should be documented and shared with the attendees afterward. Otherwise, it will be difficult to hold people accountable. For these cases, you will want to know before the meeting what the output is intended to be.

Also, confirm with your manager who will be in charge of writing the minutes, in what style (if unsure, ask for an example), and in what level of detail. You can safely assume that he or she is going to ask you to prepare a draft, which he or she will then review and send out to the meeting attendees. Thus, give your top effort here (I know, these are *just* minutes, but they are critical).

- **Confirm logistics:** Make sure you know the meeting location. Do you know how to get there? Will other people have to provide you access? Equally important, will all attendees have access or do you need to register them up front (e.g., external visitors)? When in the room, confirm that all the equipment you will need is available and fully functioning. This includes telephones, projectors, Internet connection, felt-tip pens for the whiteboard, flip-charts with sufficient paper, etc. Always test the material. Assume nothing! You want to avoid running from room to room to find working felt-tip pens once the meeting is underway.

- **Come prepared:** Come equipped to every meeting, however small and informal it may be. At all times, have pen and paper with you. It is also good practice to read up on the topic of the meeting. As a meeting organizer, you also want to have your laptop with you. You might not need it during the actual meeting if you take notes on paper, but it will come in handy when you need to project a presentation, print additional copies, or access the web or corporate address book quickly. If there are any documents to be discussed or reviewed, take several printed copies along. You will then be able to share the material with those attendees who might not have had a chance to review the material earlier. In case you are organizing a longer meeting (e.g., a workshop), which might involve some brainstorming or other group activity, check with your manager if a facilitator's kit will be required.

- **Have contact details for the attendees:** Whatever can go wrong will eventually go wrong. You might have key people not show up at the meeting. The group might realize that someone else should have been invited. Or perhaps some other third party should have briefly provided the latest stats or their view on an unanticipated discussion point. As a junior, you might be asked to reach out to certain people immediately. To act quickly (but calmly) in such situations, have the contact information of all key attendees readily available. Access to your corporate address book and any other relevant information is vital.

- **Come early:** Be in front of or in the meeting room at least ten to fifteen minutes before the official start time. When in the room, stay close to the host. To be on the safe side, casually tell your manager that you will go down to the meeting room fifteen minutes prior to the start, and ask if you should take something along on his or her behalf. This will demonstrate that you are thinking ahead and also offers your manager the opportunity to kindly inform you to go earlier, if need be.

- **Align with your manager:** Before you leave for the meeting, check with your manager on how he or she would like to run the meeting and what role you should fulfill. Don't be too proud to ask; take initiative and show that you're engaged!

DURING THE MEETING

When the meeting starts, you will likely be relegated to a less prominent role. You may be introduced, but then again, you may not. For now, don't worry. Give your best in accomplishing the tasks assigned to you. Your time to shine will come. For now, focus on the following during the meeting:

- **Reach out to missing attendees:** You expect a certain number of people to attend. Rest assured, there will always be surprises, and the group will probably be waiting for some key party. Taking care of the follow-up is the expectation for juniors. Use the contact details that you have readily available.

- **Don't tighten the screws of the projector:** Most formal meetings make use of a projector. While you will likely be asked to affix the projector to your laptop, do not turn the little screws on the plug. It often happens that laptops get swapped during meetings—often unexpectedly and more than once.

- **Listen and observe:** Be conscious of what is going on in the entire meeting room. Do not get too fixated on the host and the current speaker only. As a true supporter to a meeting host, try to pay attention to things that he or

she might miss. If some attendees are clearly not participating and mentally checking out, find ways to include
them. As this will likely be beyond your competence in
the beginning (it comes with experience), a paper note
to your manager will typically suffice. Of course, this
will vary depending on circumstances. Be pragmatic in
your approach.

- **Take notes:** By now, you should have an exact idea of
  what the required output of the meeting is. Even if you
  are not asked to write minutes, make it a habit to take
  notes. This will not only enhance your understanding
  and recollection of the content of the meeting, but it will
  also sharpen your note-taking skills for when you are actually put in charge of compiling minutes. Detailed guidance on how to write effective meeting minutes can be
  found in this book's free bonus material.

- **Share your printed copies:** In at least 75 percent of all
  meetings (based on experience, not exact science), some
  attendees will not have key documents with them. Furthermore, they have often not read critical material beforehand. You might not officially be put in charge of doing so, but there is an unwritten rule that meeting hosts
  have a handful of spare copies with them. When you notice that someone lacks the required material, proactively share the copies that you brought along. Your manager
  and the attendee in question will be grateful.

AFTER THE MEETING

Organizing a meeting does not finish when the actual meeting has
been concluded. For those in charge, there is more to be done once
all the attendees have left, such as:

- **Clean up the room:** Don't leave anything behind. Help clean up the room. This includes disposing of any loose papers and confidential material, clearing whiteboards (after having taken a photograph for your records), removing used tableware, etc.

- **Share minutes:** Depending on what you agreed on with the meeting host, you might have already been put in charge of preparing a write-up of the key discussion points and decisions made during the meeting. Otherwise, offer to prepare a write-up of the key takeaways—even if your manager might have told you differently before. Priorities may change, so your manager might appreciate this additional help now. This is also why you want to take notes at all times. You simply do not know how things will turn out. If you are put in charge of compiling minutes, confirm with the host what the exact output format and timeline should be. You will likely be asked to turn this around within twenty-four hours.

This section laid out how to *help* organize a meeting as a junior-level resource. Before we look at what you should do when you are invited to a meeting, there is one more caveat. At times, you may be completely on your own, but don't panic. The above steps still apply even though you won't have much, if any, guidance. Following the steps is a good start. The key is to have a solid agenda and work from there. If need be, reach out to one of your colleagues for additional guidance.

PARTICIPATING DURING A MEETING

When you are invited to meetings, ensure that you understand your role as potentially the least experienced person on the attendee list. This does not mean that you come for the nibbles only. In the beginning of your career, people, particularly direct superiors, will watch you carefully. If you take the following guidance to heart, you will be on the right track.

Before the Meeting

Before you attend a meeting, you have some administrative homework to complete. While this will not change greatly over the course of your career, you will require less preparation time as you become more experienced. Until then, make every effort to closely adhere to the following principles.

- **Confirm logistics:** Prior to the meeting, make sure you know its exact location. Do you know how to get there? Will other people have to provide you access? If you are unsure of these answers, reach out to the organizer or other colleagues that you trust.

- **Prepare:** Never come to a meeting unprepared. You should not only know the purpose of the meeting but also read all documents relevant to the meeting.

- **Bring useful material:** Come equipped to every meeting, however small and informal. Always have pen and paper with you as this conveys readiness and a willingness to engage. If there are documents to be discussed, take printed copies along.

- **Come early:** Be at the meeting venue at least five minutes before the official start. As you are a junior resource, do not grab a seat right away. Remain standing until someone else has sat down. You want to avoid a) being the first one to sit and b) sitting in the wrong place. Yes, there are wrong places. Ideally, you should ask if it is okay to sit next to someone that you know or with whom you feel comfortable. If it is a small group, sit across the table, but always consider whether very senior people are yet to arrive. You want to avoid them having to sit far away either from the group or the phone (in case other people are dialing in). If you find this is too prescriptive, talk to those who have put their foot in the mouth in the past.

DURING THE MEETING

During the meeting, you are probably not required to say much, if anything, at all. For juniors, meetings are not the right platform to speak up, especially if you have nothing meaningful to contribute. However, remember that people are watching you, so you should do the following:

- **Listen:** Adopt an active listening style. Do not sit back and let time pass by. Instead, convey the impression that you are closely following what is being discussed. This does not require contributing more than frequent nods to the speaker and a genuine smile. Having said this, if you are able to contribute to the discussion, by all means do so.

- **Take notes:** Apart from an active listening style, you want to take notes. This will not only enhance your understanding and recollection of the content of the meeting but will also make a good impression on those keeping an eye on you.

AFTER THE MEETING

When the meeting is over, you could simply leave and get on with your own business, which is what most people do. That being said, you should try to stand out and lead by example from early on. There is no right or wrong here. The precise steps you could take depend on the context, but consider the below points and choose what makes the most sense in your specific case.

- **Leave your seat spotless:** At the very least, leave it the same way that you found it at the start of the meeting. If your schedule allows, help clean up the room. This includes disposing of loose papers and confidential material, clearing whiteboards, removing used tableware, etc.

- **Offer your help:** Provided that the meeting was conducted effectively, participants should have agreed on a number of follow-up actions. Seek ways to support if you can, but don't dig your own grave either. In other words, don't jump on every opportunity. Because while hard work is a great start, to a large degree, success is also "about working on the right things."[20]

- **Connect with people:** Take time for small talk, if feasible. Again, use common sense here. Do not waste other people's time, and avoid being seen as having nothing else to do.

A Primer on Meeting Invitations

As with anything at work, you want to be efficient. Given that there are few shortcuts for juniors, at least avoid trying to reinvent the wheel again and again. There is not much of a difference between sending invitations for meetings or telephone conferences, as discussed in the previous chapter.

In fact, the key differences may be whether you will have people dial in, in addition to those attending in person. If that's the case, simply add dial-in details as you would normally do in telephone conference invitations.

However, do not add dial-in details by default. You will not know who is going to attend in person and who might dial in. If people unexpectedly require dial-in details for a meeting, let them reach out to you directly.

EXAMPLE MEETING INVITATION

In Project Insight, the team has run into some initial challenges. Data quality from the Birmingham warehouse is very poor (which is surprisingly often the case in large organizations), and they are struggling to find time with GLT's operations analyst, Andrew Seagull. Mark is asked to schedule a brief meeting with Robert Grant, GTL's Project Lead, to discuss immediate issue resolution (Table 7).

You could use the above example as a template for your "meeting invites." I only set this up after having rewritten invites hundreds of times in my first year. Note that as long as you have not been officially introduced, you will likely not send out the actual invitation. Meeting requests from unknown senders are usually discarded or handled with less urgency.

While setting up meetings, you will inevitably run into difficulties. Some people will not be available, others will not respond, etc. Keep track of your progress and proactively provide feedback to your manager. This will allow you to cover yourself and let your manager jump in, if need be.

WHEN YOU ARE THE RECIPIENT OF A MEETING INVITATION

If you are the recipient of a meeting request, there are a number of things you should immediately check.

- Do you understand the purpose of the meeting request? Are the objectives and intended outcomes clear to you? If

Area	Example	Comment
To:	R Grant (Project Lead GTL) M Perez (Project Lead FT)	All those required belong to the "To:" section. Mark also needs to do this in the right order, i.e., external client staff from senior to junior, internal staff from senior to junior.
Cc:	J Cazeneuve (Project Sponsor GTL) P Jackson (CEO FT)	Optional attendees can be cc'd. Manuela Perez instructed Mark to cc both GTL project sponsor and the FT's CEO. This is to keep them in the loop about potential risks. It is unlikely for them to attend for such details, but they should be aware of them in any event.
Subject line	Project Insight: Discuss Initial Challenges & Remedies	The subject line should be short and relevant. The purpose of the meeting should be clear from the subject line. Mark mentions the project, and topic.
Location	FT Boston, Room 251	From the location field the recipients should easily know where the meeting takes place. In the event of people dialing in corresponding dial-in codes will have to be provided here.
Body	Dear all, Hereby I am scheduling a brief 30-min. meeting on Project Insight. The objective of the meeting is to: • Update on progress made and challenges encountered • Address data quality issues • Arrange additional temporary support to Andrew In case this time does not suit you, please let me know (by providing two alternative time slots). Best, Mark **Contact Details** Mark Johnson Mobile: +1 123 445 445 Email: m.johnson@futuretech.com	This email body assumes Mark has done his homework and confirmed key people will be able to attend. You want to be as specific as possible. If there are certain documents to be reviewed or discussed, mention this here, too. You want to require people to reach out to you in case they cannot join. Depending on your style or standing in the organization, you may request alternative time slots be provided when declining the invite. Adding your signature is key. Make it easy for people to contact you directly from the invite. This includes at a minimum your cell phone number and email address.

Table 7: Meeting Invitation

not, follow up with the organizer by replying directly and only to the sender (i.e., do not use "Reply All" in this case).

- Will this meeting be back to back with another meeting in your agenda? If so, can you reschedule the one of lower importance? If both are already locked in and cannot be moved, contact the organizer of the preceding meeting (unless it is your boss or an external client) to check whether you can step out five minutes early to allow you to attend the second meeting. If this is not possible, turn to the organizer of the meeting whose invitation you have just received and inform him or her that you will likely be five minutes late due to an earlier meeting.

Key Takeaways

- Don't buy into popular advice on how to avoid meetings. As a junior, you are not in the position to decide whether you attend or not unless there are critical business needs that are more important than your presence.

- See the bigger picture. There is more to meetings than the actual gathering of stakeholders in a room. Juniors can (and are expected to) support well before, during, and after the meeting.

- Give your best in terms of meeting organization. You might not play a prominent role during the meeting, but both preparatory and post-processing work provide plenty of opportunities to shine.

- Always come prepared. Whatever the meeting is that you are attending, ensure that you have thoroughly prepared. Never take this lightly.

- Leverage what you already have. Meeting invitations lend themselves to be set up as standard templates. Only adjust dates and discussion points to save time.

[9]

Managing Your Time

> *"My favorite things in life don't cost any money. It's really clear that the most precious resource we all have is time."*

Steve Jobs

ACCORDING TO JODY THOMPSON and Cali Ressler, the pioneers of ROWE (Results-Only Work Environment), "When people have high demands and low control, their life is both hectic and miserable.... The challenge then is to increase your level of control so you can effectively meet demands."[21] This chapter is supposed to give you back a bit more of that control. Whether you work primarily with external or internal clients, you will likely experience various time constraints. You will also have a hard time finding shortcuts at first. Certain processes performed at a junior level may be automated, but the majority won't.

Therefore, the question is how to make the most of the time you have available, noting that you will have limited bargaining power and, like in most organizations, your client will (almost) always be right. In addition, you probably want to try to manage both business and private matters simultaneously. You won't be the first to do so.

However, the odds are against you unless you have some simple, consistent systems in place.

The next two sections will be all about how you can navigate your work environment and deliver good quality outputs on time without losing sight of your own personal matters. First, we will review how you can put yourself in a good position when starting a job through expectation management. We will then look more closely at how you can manage your tasks effectively in any given period of time.

The Art of Expectation Management

In order to minimize the noise directed at you, namely in the form of follow-ups and interruptions, you should establish some ground rules before working on any type of job. You will need to align with your senior colleagues on the scope of work, deadlines, and regular checkpoints. A lack thereof will backfire. So how do you go about this?

Agree on the Scope of Work

The scope of work describes what your final deliverable should include and potentially how to get there. Although it might be difficult in the beginning to estimate the actual steps necessary to accomplish a task, try to be as specific as possible with your manager. It also helps to agree with your manager about what you are not going to do in this process.

For example, think of our financial analyst, Mark Johnson of Future Technologies. He would have two completely different starting points if asked to:

- Analyze sales in Europe (poor)

- Analyze the sales of Product X in countries A, B, and C, including list price and discounts per item per customer, from 2012–2015 for all sales channels (better)

Agree on Deadlines

Before starting to work on an assignment, you should agree on a deadline. No exceptions. It does not matter if a request to you is being made by email, by phone, or in person. Always respond by asking this key question:

"By when would you need this back at the latest?"

The person asking for your help will often play the ball back to you. Use this to your advantage. The agreed upon deadline should be in your favor. If being asked how long it will take, do not try to impress the person by offering too short of a turnaround time. Instead, aim for a timeframe that gives you sufficient leeway in case you run into obstacles. Also, be sure to challenge unrealistic expectations.

Furthermore, don't try to deliver something overnight unless it is absolutely necessary. If you receive a request by 6 p.m., you do not have to deliver the work by 8 a.m. Usually, it is sufficient to deliver by 12 p.m. the next day unless indicated differently. This should be common sense, but I have seen many juniors (and seniors) forget this.

Provide Frequent Updates

You might have agreed on the scope and deadline with your manager. Now what? Do not rush ahead and avoid updating your manager until the deadline. Your manager will have sleepless nights unless you keep him or her in the loop. No one likes surprises (at work), especially not bad ones.

Provide informal updates either verbally (if you share a room) or by email when you have something to report. This includes both minor accomplishments (within reason) and potential challenges.

If your manager asks you how things are going, you have failed to provide the right amount of updates. Adapt your style to your manager. This will become easier over time. For starters, make it a habit to provide more short updates than you actually feel are necessary. Err on the side of too much communication versus too little. Your manager can do with too many updates rather than too few. If in doubt, simply ask whether he or she felt comfortable with the amount of updates provided so as to avoid any potential criticism when performance feedback comes around.

The purpose of these updates is to inform your manager about your progress. As such, you should be completely honest about how you're doing. If you need help or more time, flag this early. Do not start on an assignment on Monday that is expected by Friday at 12 p.m. only to realize at 10 a.m. on Friday that you cannot meet the deadline.

Effective Task Management

Assuming that you have agreed on a basic understanding with your manager regarding the scope and timeline of a certain job, you will now want to work toward accomplishing the same. By now, you also understand that priorities may shift instantly, and sticking to your personal timeline may be difficult in practice. Therefore, we shall look at some task management principles as they pertain to junior-level resources and highlight both the pitfalls and potential remedies.

To-Do Lists and Chunking

Whatever system you use to manage your tasks, it should be simple and enable you to focus on getting things done. Your approach is not a goal in and of itself. You will want to focus on action and less on the process. Don't spend too much time thinking through your approach once you have settled on one. Otherwise, you run the risk of decision fatigue, which describes the gradual deterioration of your decision-making power.

Your mind is like a muscle. The more often you use it, the stronger it gets. However, just like any muscle, it will suffer from fatigue when used excessively. Exercising for an entire day isn't conducive to health, and it's the same with making decisions. According to research from Columbia University,[22] this sort of fatigue can have a measurable negative impact on the quality of your decision-making skills and willpower.

So how can we accommodate this? We need a simple system to structure our day-to-day responsibilities in order to reduce the number of low-impact decisions that need to be made during the day. In other words, you want to avoid thinking, "What next?" over and over again, and save mental brainpower for decisions that matter.

What seems to work best for high-achievers in any industry when working toward their goals is using to-do lists. Why? Because they are simple and they work. Composing a to-do list requires you to come up with an action plan of how to tackle the tasks at hand. You will have to consider your approach and give structure to what might seem chaotic. To accomplish this, prioritization is paramount. Once done, you will rarely have to decide again what to tackle next. Try to focus on completing each task consecutively, one after the other. If possible, do not switch between tasks. While sometimes this is inevitable, multitasking kills productivity[23] (and can even reduce your IQ).[24]

If you have trouble prioritizing your tasks, consider using the Eisenhower Matrix, popularized by Stephen Covey.[25] It provides a simple framework to distinguish the important from the unimportant.

In addition, apply rigorous chunking (or clustering) to your to-do list. Group whatever can be grouped. Similar tasks should be performed together. For example, making different calls can be clustered and executed as a session of calls, etc.

Here's one final caveat: get comfortable with change. You should structure your day, but priorities may change during any given day, based on urgent business needs. Therefore, you had better develop a certain degree of flexibility. That applies to all employment levels but is particularly important when you are just starting out.

Forget Electronic Sticky Notes . . .

. . . Unless your boss is using them too. It is strongly recommended to work off paper-based to-do lists and forgo those electronic sticky notes on your screen. As mentioned before, you will have to earn trust from your colleagues. Chances are that one of your colleagues, for better or worse, will (subconsciously) question your reliability when getting the job done. You can mitigate this by being extremely transparent in your work. Always be willing to share your progress with your team. Paper-based to-do lists serve that purpose because they are visible.

I once made the mistake of completely working off a to-do list that I was keeping on my machine. It was very convenient for me, as we were commuting between client sites frequently. However, I took a hit afterward when my performance review came around. As part of the feedback provided, I was asked to "learn how to use to-do lists." Upon questioning this remark, I learned that my manager had not seen any to-do lists on my desk and, putting two and two together, assumed that I had not kept any log at all.

While I did not really buy into the feedback, I immediately changed my approach and started writing down my daily to-do list on paper. Every job that required my attention and was finished got crossed off. I was very liberal in what I called a "job," because it did not really matter. The important thing was having visibly crossed off items on my list. Finished something that was not on the list before? Put it on the list and cross it off right away. It also felt great (i.e., a dopamine release).

Does this sound like a lot of nonsense? Perhaps, but I have never received the same feedback since, and plenty of my colleagues have adopted a similar approach.

SCHEDULE RECURRING EVENTS OR ACTIVITIES

Those people who get a lot done are usually no smarter than anyone else. They have simply structured their tasks in a way that allows them to focus. "Follow standard routines to minimize the mundane aspects of life so you can concentrate on what's most important to you," senior lecturer at Harvard Business School and former executive Bob Pozen recommends.[26] Many recurring tasks lend themselves to be scheduled on a weekly, monthly, or quarterly basis, such as:

- Entering your hours worked in a reporting system (weekly)

- Filing your expenses (weekly/monthly) (if applicable)

- Fulfilling compliance requirements (as required)

- Meeting with your mentor (monthly/quarterly)

- Considering professional training options (quarterly);

I recommend that you schedule these events early on. The whole process takes less than five minutes.

SPLIT BUSINESS AND PRIVATE MATTERS

If you have not used to-do lists for private matters until now, then by all means consider starting. If you already do this, be careful not to mix up business and private concerns. How can you effectively go about that? Anything related to your business will take precedence unless some private matter is absolutely vital. You might disagree on that point, but that's understandable. I'm just sharing what works for me and others. Anything else is up to you.

I suggest you keep two separate to-do lists (see Table 8). Ideally, you should have a different format for each. All your work tasks will be put on paper for the reasons outlined above. Your private stuff should be captured elsewhere. You will want to take the exact opposite approach with your private business and limit transparen-

	Business	**Private**
Objective	Visibility	Confidentiality
	Transparency	Privacy
Tool	Paper-based to-do list (potentially supported with task tracker in MS Excel)	Computer-based task management application (e.g., Wunderlist)

Table 8: Business vs. Private To-Do Lists

cy to your colleagues as much as possible. Your manager is not the right person to learn that you have to book flights during work hours, make an appointment with your hairdresser, or call your bank.

Don't get me wrong. Everyone does these kinds of things. For example, try calling a bank on the weekend . . . Even though everyone engages in the same behavior, don't provide any potential target for cheap feedback from more experienced folks. Therefore, I recommend managing your private to-do list online. Access this list at any time from your browser. I use Wunderlist,[27] which synchronizes across multiple platforms, making it easy to manage my private to-do list on the go, but there are also many other tools available.

Finally, it should be clear by now that chunking is the way to go for to-do lists. What works in business matters also works well in private matters. Schedule recurring reminders to make financial transactions or take private calls. Wherever possible, schedule those to-do items on the weekend. Keep your week free at first, unless it is an emergency (which probably would not be captured in a to-do list to begin with). You will appreciate every bit of flexibility you have maintained during a busy workday. Don't let "buying milk" get in the way of that.

A Dry Run: How to Manage To-Do Lists

Let's take a look at the concrete steps that I recommend you take when managing your different lists (see Figure 8). First, I will describe a practical weekly routine. Afterward, I will explain how you can best focus on daily execution.

Your Weekly Routine

Every Sunday night, you will want to set yourself up for another week of success, but this requires preparation. Make it a habit (*read*: put a reminder in your calendar right now) to think ahead and consider what the key milestones of the upcoming week will be. Do this for all major pieces of work or projects in which you are involved.

Ideally, this will only require a short review of existing tasks that you have identified for yourself. You might need to consider certain changes in timing, but other than that, you should be ready to go. At times, you will derive certain tasks from new business developments that might not have been on your radar before. Capture those and then enjoy the last few hours of your weekend with a glass of your preferred wine.

Figure 8: Weekly To-Do List Management Cycle

Your Daily Routine

Before you start your workday, you should establish a good understanding of your tasks as they currently stand and the potential challenges that might occur throughout the day. Review your daily to-do list first thing. Identify the key tasks to be accomplished and get started. Focus your efforts on the most important and urgent tasks first.

There is one caveat: Before thinking about work just after waking up, do something that matters to you personally. For example, a standard morning routine consisting of exercise, reading, doing yoga, or learning a language can lay the foundation for a happier and more productive day. Don't schedule it for "sometime later." That time will never come. It is far too easy to "call it a day" because of exhaustion at 10 p.m.

Once at work, don't sweat the small stuff immediately.[28] These might be quick wins, but they likely don't matter in the grand scheme of things. There will be plenty of short stints of downtime during which you can take care of minor tasks. Again, this will not save you from changing course during the day, but it will help you manage the demands put on you much more easily. Before finishing the day, review your list of open items once again. Ideally, there are none, which is rare in most high-performance organizations. Think ahead to the next day "at the circus" and get some rest.

Two Renegade Tactics to Get Your Sanity Back

Many people interviewed for this book have shared effective and often very original time management tactics. Keep in mind, those measures are not recommended to be used in your first year (or even during your probation period). To be on the safe side, you want to have gained a certain degree of positive reputation before using either of the following two tactics.

The Meeting for One

If you are particularly busy and struggle to get things done, consider blocking time in your own agenda. An effective way to do this is simply booking meetings with yourself in your calendar. In many corporations, people can view each other's availability. Thus, you would appear to be in a meeting, i.e., unavailable, while you are actually working hard to accomplish your own tasks.

Granted, those calendar entries do not have to last for an entire afternoon. If a 30-minute session of undisturbed focus should be all you need to finalize that project plan, then why not give yourself the time you need and still keep your day on track?

The Extra Holiday Hack

Before you start your holidays—or any other extended period away from work—you should set up an out-of-office message. This is what people will receive when they send you an email while you are traveling; 99% of the time, people indicate in that message when they are going to be back at work. This is definitely a best practice. Essentially, you should let the sender know when they can expect a response.

However, here is the problem. If I send you an email and get the response that you are going to return on Monday, 12 September 2016, guess what I am going to do? Schedule a follow-up for exactly that day (either by phone or email). A better approach for you would be to inform senders (here, me) that you are going to be back on Tuesday, effectively one day later. This will allow you to have a smooth start after your break, rather than having to juggle dozens of incoming (follow-up) calls and emails. Don't leave your manager and close colleagues in doubt; confirm your true date of return with them.

Bonus: Unleash Hidden IT Powers

Effective time management strategies are key. But don't underestimate the importance of minute adjustments either. At times, small changes can have significant impact over the long haul. For starters, I recommend you reduce the reaction time of your keyboard and increase the tracking speed of your track pad (or mouse). Break the chains of your desk work! Many of the people interviewed for this book agree that these changes have significantly sped up their day-to-day work. Try it! It might take a day to get used to, but I promise you won't go back to the default.

Key Takeaways

♦ Work smarter. You might have little leeway in how you structure your workday. Therefore, efficiency-enhancing time management techniques are vital to cope with typical time constraints.

♦ Manage your senior's expectations. Agree on the scope and deadline of a task before you get to work. Provide regular progress updates to avoid taking your manager by surprise.

♦ Use to-do lists. Capture all tasks assigned in groups of similar activities. This allows you to work efficiently and ensures that you do not lose track of your progress.

♦ Separate private matters from business tasks. Personal action items should not get in the way of accomplishing your work. Schedule them elsewhere, ideally on the weekend.

♦ Regularly review your to-do lists. Conduct weekly reviews on Sunday to plan the upcoming week. Every day, review the tasks for that day in the morning and when closing the day so that you remain on top of things.

[10]

Staying Ahead

> *"Endless Newbie is the new default for everyone,*
> *no matter your age or experience."*
>
> **Kevin Kelly, *The Inevitable***

WHEN YOU START YOUR career, you might have just graduated from one of the major business schools. Chances are,
you were also at the top of your class. If you think that after years of learning, you can now focus on practically applying your
knowledge, I've got news for you: the real learning starts now.

In this chapter, I will highlight why continuous learning is not
just a fancy concept in textbooks and why it matters today more than
ever. Before we consider what you should focus on personally, you
will learn about the different roads you can take to enhance your
skill set in general. Afterwards, we will discuss what I perceive as
the two most important daily habits to succeed in the learning game.
We will conclude the chapter by making a case for speaking foreign
languages, despite the fact that English is now the global language
of business.

Continuous Learning is Not a Buzzword

As explained in Chapter 1, to employers, you are valuable in two ways: experience and skills. Unfortunately, at the beginning of your career, you have almost none of the former and little of the latter. Gaining experience only comes with time. You cannot force it overnight, although you can seek out environments that help you gain experience faster. What you can influence directly is your skill set.

Get a degree, secure a well-paying job, and start your career. That has worked for previous generations, but it no longer holds true. According to best-selling author and career expert Michael Ellsberg, "More and more people [...] are waking up to the reality that the old career and success advice is no longer adequate."[29] Graduating from university is only an entry ticket into the job market, and lifelong employment is a thing of the past. Yes, there are those who have 30 or more years of tenure in big corporations, but they make up a dying breed. For the rest of us, the workplace is rapidly evolving. "Handle the challenge of change well, and you can prosper greatly. Handle it poorly, and you put yourself and others at risk,"[30] say management thought leaders Kotter and Rathgeber. From management and organizational practices to technology being used, change is the only constant.

The software developer cannot be complacent with the programming skills he acquired five years ago, but must constantly be up to date. The international marketing professional might benefit from learning about cultural peculiarities or foreign languages, as being multi-culturally competent is a core skill in this day and age[31]—not only in the marketing profession. The sales professional can no longer hold on to his Rolodex; sophisticated CRM tools are the norm. Likewise, discounts for loyal clients can no longer be based on gut feelings; pricing analytics are key in order to stay in business.

Social philosopher Eric Hoffer argued that "in a time of drastic change, it is the learners who inherit the future."[32] No matter where you look, continuous learning and development are crucial. Enhancing your skills should therefore be your priority. "Most of what you'll need to learn to be successful you'll have to learn on your own,"[33] says Ellsberg. And strategy expert Robert Greene adds, "You must value learning above everything else."[34] You do this by continuously keeping your knowledge and skills fresh. You need to grow in whatever role you fill. This is particularly true if you have increasing responsibility, because today's capabilities won't be sufficient for tomorrow's requirements.

However, it does not stop there. You also have to really "breathe" your industry, and understand what makes it tick. Industry trends, latest insights, you name it. Ultimately, this will make the difference between whether you are employable or not—in every sense of the word. Are you useful to your current employer? Would you be a valuable product in the marketplace, i.e., would others hire you? You have to demonstrate that you are on top of things and that you are sharp. Ideally, you have succeeded in or are beginning to succeed in delivering tangible value from your ongoing learning.

Fortunately, you do not have to figure things out all by yourself. There are plenty of learning resources available. Let us review what these are, and how to take advantage of them in the best possible way.

RESOURCES AVAILABLE TO YOU

How do you continuously upgrade your skills? There are many ways, but by and large they fall into one of three categories. First, there is learning on the job, which is learning through first-hand experience. This is by far the most effective method of sharpening skills for most people. Whether you are simply trying new (better) approaches in your day-to-day job, taking on more challenging assignments, volunteering on short-term engagements with other departments (see

Chapter 13), covering for colleagues when they are on leave, supporting (or mentoring) more junior team members to help them develop, or standing in for more senior colleagues in meetings when they are unavailable.... Ultimately, all these experiences will help you perform better on your current level. However, they also lay the building blocks for transitioning to the next step on the corporate ladder. Thus, having experience in various contexts is vital to your development.

Second, you can learn from and through other people. Here, you can think of colleagues you consider role models, mentors, coaches, or any other person you look up to. It is important to be proactive when you want to learn from other people. Solely observing is unlikely to be enough. Instead, you should make an effort to work together more often with colleagues who are good at the skill you want to develop, request specific feedback on areas you want to develop (see Chapter 14), or ask someone to mentor you (see Chapter 12). Besides, there may be situations in which you can even learn from the exact opposite type of person, those who you do not look up to in any way. You might be able to identify certain behaviors or strategies that are not effective, and adjust yourself accordingly.

Gaining first-hand experience and learning from other people both have one thing in common: the effectiveness of either path, in terms of enhancing your skills, is not completely in your hands. You should seek out opportunities to learn from both, but not everyone is fortunate enough to work in an environment that allows for either (or both) to provide substantial benefits to personal development.

Therefore, let us focus more on what is actually in your hands: the application of learning resources. Given the importance of a skilled workforce, many companies provide a wide range of learning opportunities. Granted, few things are more useful than practical learning on the job, but do not just wait and hope for the learning to occur. Be proactive (if only in your free time) because you have plenty of learning resources, both internal and external, to select from.

INTERNAL RESOURCES

Internal resources are all those knowledge resources you can access via your corporate network. At times, there are restrictions (e.g., eligibility for certain levels only), but for the most part, they are all there and ready for you to grasp when you choose to spend time on them.

- **Internal course catalogue:** Almost all companies offer regular courses for their staff. These are often grade-specific and are either run by external facilitators or more senior staff. The courses offered can be anywhere between two hours and multiple days. While dependent on your industry, expect anything from structured thinking, presentation design, business writing, and financial modeling to programming. This is particularly valuable for those starting out (you!), as they lay the professional foundation that you will be working from going forward.

- **Online course:** Major industry players usually provide their employees with a vast amount of online trainings via the company's intranet. Content ranges from professional skill development to enhancing industry-specific knowledge. As some of the material may be a bit dated at times, it is probably best to ask more experienced colleagues or people from the learning team (if available) for their recommendations.

- **Knowledge-sharing platform:** Depending on the importance of past deliverables (e.g., proposals in a sales organization), you might have access to some shared knowledge repository. Sometimes, information contained will be cleansed, meaning that anything that can be traced back to a specific client (name, logo, color schemes, etc.) has been removed. Not all the information will be relevant, but you can often learn a thing or two about how others have solved a certain problem that you are facing. In case your company does not share knowledge systematically, try to initiate and implement some type of knowledge-sharing system for your own team.

External Resources

External resources are all those knowledge resources that lie outside your corporate network. As such, you will have to do initial research yourself and, most likely, invest some of your personal time and money. However, this does not mean that you will not get reimbursed or receive some support from your employer. There is always a chance to negotiate something, provided that 1) you ask (most people fail here) and 2) you can clearly articulate the value of your work.

- **Newspapers and magazines:** Scan the news every day. You do not need to study everything in depth, but make sure that you have a solid understanding of what is happening in the "real" world, especially with respect to your industry. You can subscribe to professional news feeds covering specific companies and industries via most corporate networks.

- **Books:** Books are the most accessible knowledge resource you can utilize. Standing on the shoulders of giants has never been easier since books are now available in formats for all tastes (print, e-book, audiobook). Make it a habit to keep a reading list at all times. If you do not know where to start, order the five most relevant books in the professional field you are starting in right now and work your way through them over the next few weeks. Do not let a month pass without having read a new book (no matter how busy and intense your schedule may be). If that sounds too difficult, sign up with getabstract.com.

For less than the cost of a nice dinner for two, you will get a year's worth of access to thousands of concise summaries of both classic and recent publications. You might also want to check whether your employer has a corporate account with this sort of platform that is available for employees.

- **Online resources:** These days, there is next to nothing that you can't learn via the Internet. Whatever obscure interest you may have, there is bound to be a community of enthusiasts online. The easiest starting point remains YouTube, especially when it comes to how-to pieces related to technical skills. YouTube almost always has some useful information to get you started. TED talks are another useful source of information. While they may not help you solve immediate technical problems, they can still broaden your horizons and sharpen your thinking. Make it a habit to regularly watch TED talks at ted.com when you have downtime (e.g., during breakfast or dinner). If you are looking for more in-depth courses online, check out online academies like Udemy. There, you can find information on anything from office productivity (Office, SAP, SalesForce, etc.), project management, and data analytics to IT certifications and more. Selecting from the 20,000+ courses is the hardest part.

- **Other external professional courses:** Every once in a while you might realize that your corporate network does not provide training on a certain topic. If you consider this critical to your own development, conduct some research on who delivers this type of training and at what price point you could join. With thorough information and a clear case for why a training is business-critical, you can discuss and agree on the next steps with your mentor. Do not simply rush ahead and put this on your boss's agenda. Your mentor can guide you in terms of the best approach and might show you funding options of which you had been unaware. In case you can't secure funding from your company, consider whether it makes sense to go ahead and personally pay for the training anyway. In the rush of day-to-day business, training often gets forgotten or deprioritized. Don't let this happen to you. Remember, today's learning will lead to tomorrow's reward.

Ultimately, you should just focus on getting better professionally and personally. If you attend courses, never take part only for the certificate. At times, they may be required for promotions, but they do not matter in the grand scheme of things. However, learning and developing yourself do matter—a lot.

Your Own Development Journey or What to Focus On

Continuous learning is important—at all levels. This is particularly true in your early career, as it is very much about personal development at this stage. But what areas do you focus on?

Your Personal SWOT Analysis

Most people excel at one thing, and don't excel at another. The hard part is figuring out what those are in your case. Are you great with numbers? Can you talk well in public? Are you born for sales? Do a personal SWOT analysis. What works for businesses can be applied to careers too. "Begin by systematically developing rare and valuable skills," says career expert Cal Newport.[35] Whatever the core skill is that comes to you naturally, your career will be boosted when you recognize your strengths and seek opportunities that play to them. If leveraged effectively, your unique skill set forms the foundation for your personal brand. That means you should also let people know what you are good at. This can really set your career in motion. After all, it often goes like this: visibility, recognition, consideration, progress. Therefore, identify your strengths and master them (and spread the message).

Most likely, you will also notice certain areas where you could improve. If not, expect others to point them out sooner or later. Where these are critical to your work, you have to take action quickly. They can be very technical, but they don't have to be. Whatever the shortcoming is, if it is relevant to your job, there is no justification not to strive for improvement when you are starting out.

COMMON AREAS OF IMPROVEMENT

In case you are in doubt about areas that you can focus on improving, consider the following. Based on the interviews conducted for this book, typical areas of improvement for juniors include:

- Communication (e.g., how to communicate effectively with customers or senior executives, how to have difficult conversations with your manager)

- Presentation (e.g., how to develop and deliver effective business presentations, storytelling)

- Project management (e.g., how to manage multiple stakeholders and work streams, project plans, and budgets)

- General problem-solving and analytical skills

- Other technical skills (specific to your work)

- Other soft skills, including working in teams (across different locations), collaborating with people you do not like, managing (other junior) people (e.g., interns)

How to Truly Stay Ahead

By now, you can probably appreciate why continuous learning is the name of game for today's career starters. It is the very foundation of your work. You will also have gained an understanding of what type of learning resources are available to you. All of this needs to be put into practice, and even then, you are likely only doing the bare minimum. At the least, you're probably not standing out by a great margin. Is that what you have been working so hard for in the past, to be just like everybody else?

To truly get ahead—and stay there—you need to adopt key habits. Attending a training here and there will not cut it.[36] A master of any field will tell you that it is habitual and deliberate practice that makes the difference.[37] Two simple yet powerful practices that can put you on the path toward excellence will be discussed next. If adopted, I guarantee that you will benefit both professionally and privately.

Reading Yourself to Success

Reading is crucial. As the old adage goes, *if you want to become a leader, you have to be a reader.* This holds true in most professions. The problem is that most people in full-time employment do not take the time to read, but you should know better. It should be in your own self-interest to read regularly and read more. After all, reading has palpable benefits, which help build a more bulletproof career in a knowledge society.

Regardless of whether you seek to become a leading figure in your field or just want to get by, here are five ways in which you personally benefit from reading.

- **Providing context:** If you want to be able to put things into context, you need to have a basic understanding of what's going on. Yes, I am referring to basic news here. You don't need to have all the answers, but at least have a general understanding of what is happening out there in the world. For instance, I know plenty of consultants (both colleagues and competitors) who are nowhere near up to date, to put it mildly. Don't get me wrong. Technical skills and industry expertise are important, and no news snippet is worth forgoing expanding your knowledge in your own domain. However, I would argue that without being able to see all of this in the bigger picture, none of it is going to matter. Even the low-information diet proposed by Tim Ferriss[38] does not encourage complete abstinence from news. Instead, he argues in favor of a more deliberate, high-level approach to getting a basic understanding of what is going on. Being aware of current issues and being able to see connections are essential to understanding the world in which we live.

- **Broadening your horizons:** Expand your knowledge. Read material pertaining to your area of expertise, including current trends, new research, and whatever else can help sharpen your profile in your field. But don't stop there! You should also read material that is completely unknown to you. Even better, read material that is completely unknown to both you and those with whom you compete. Chances are, you will get an invaluable edge just by being able to see new connections or to come up with original ideas.

- **Challenging your own thinking:** Do not refrain from reading the opposite of what you might typically like. Read material with which you disagree. Tackle the confirmation bias of your newsfeed head-on. The reason for this is simple. In order to be able to put yourself in someone else's shoes, a certain degree of mental openness is vital. The problem is, as we grow up, we are meant to stand for something and are asked to have opinions. Choosing sides means favoring one over the other, which is not good for openness. Openness, however, is essential in the modern world.

Whether you work in multicultural teams or engage with different customers, you will eventually face challenges originating from different views of the world. Therefore, read (or at least skim through) the opposite of what you are normally interested in. If you think you will disagree with something, then you're missing the point. You are not meant to agree, simply to understand. Being aware of potential differences is the first step. When you understand the other side, you can more easily accommodate and possibly turn around a situation in your own favor—with family, friends, colleagues, and, above all, customers.

- **Kick-starting yourself:** In times of hardship or simply during the daily grind, a good read can provide strength for one's mind. In fact, it is likely one of the best things you can do to start off your day. It doesn't matter what you're into. For some, it is one of the holy books, while others prefer the latest self-help material. Another person might draw strength from philosophical classics (e.g., Seneca), and still others could find joy in reading autobiographies (e.g., Richard Branson's *Losing My Virginity*). Whatever works for you is fine, but give yourself the gift of regular time to read. It can kick-start your day or provide answers when you need them most.

- **Keeping your idea muscle working:** A recent study indicated a positive relationship between city size and the creativity of its population. However, rather than creativity increasing proportionally in a one-to-one manner, they found a consistent increase of greater than one to one (a superlinear scaling effect). "A city that was ten times larger than its neighbor wasn't ten times more innovative; it was seventeen times more innovative. A metropolis fifty times bigger than a town was 130 times more innovative."[39]

So what does this mean for you? As odd as this might sound, replicate a city for yourself. The more ideas you expose yourself to, the greater the creative benefit. While there are specific practices to enhance your fortitude in developing ideas (see the next section, "Becoming an Idea Machine"), it all starts with knowledge input. The more diverse the topics, the better. They will activate your brain and enhance your creativity. Before you know it, your capacity to come up with ideas will skyrocket. Remember, ideas are what you are being paid for. Small ideas, big ideas...it doesn't matter. Just bring something new to the table!

In a nutshell, read more. Do it regularly. Make it a habit to read thirty minutes each day if you can. Use any downtime that you may have, whether it is on the daily commute or while you're winding down after work. Don't become so immersed in your work that you forget about working on yourself. I know of many people who lacked the essential knowledge of current issues and had no idea about any new insights in their areas of expertise. Don't be like that. Being valuable means having ideas. To have ideas, you must expose yourself to new stuff—often. No, actually, do it *all the time*.

There is value in reading, and no matter how great the demands on you are at work, all of us should free up time to enhance our perspectives on the world. No one else will do it for you!

Not sure how to read more given a full agenda? In the Appendix I have listed resources that can help you read more in less time.

Becoming an Idea Machine

The second habit is to work toward becoming an idea machine. Regardless of what type of role you perform, most jobs no longer pay for mere execution. Proactivity is expected. That being said, being proactive is simple when you have a constant flow of ideas.

So, what is an idea machine? Someone who constantly comes up with ideas. No matter the situation, whether deliberately sought or not, these people are coming up with new concepts. Do all these ideas need to be groundbreaking? Of course not. With everything we practice, what we produce often makes no sense. Lots of ideas will be useless or even ridiculous. Don't limit your imagination by trying to exclusively come up with good ideas. Focus on quantity first. Quality will naturally follow.

The question is, how can you become a well of creativity? James Altucher wrote an in-depth post on how to become an idea machine.[40] Read it. In essence, take a few minutes every day and come up with ten ideas for any topic. Again, these ideas do not have to be great. To come up with a topic, just ask yourself some question. Any question will do. It could be simple, complex, random, or directly aimed at solving a very concrete problem that you are currently facing. Here are some examples:

- What are ten ways to increase team morale in my division or office?

- Which ten potential customers could benefit from the latest research conducted by my company?

- Which ten approaches could we take to attract high-caliber talent, in addition to my company's existing recruiting activities?

- What are ten additional revenue streams my customers could tap into?

- What ten things have I learned today?

I take no credit for this approach, because it belongs to James Altucher. However, I highly believe in the concept. Anyone in a knowledge-based job should do the same; check out James's blog at JamesAltucher.com or order his book.[41]

ARE WE SPEAKING THE SAME LANGUAGE?

In one of my first consulting projects, we had to interact with stakeholders from across Europe. For one reason or another, we encountered a number of challenges liaising with the client team in France. We were somewhat puzzled, since our relationships with other country teams were flawless. At some point, another colleague jumped in during someone's vacation. Despite being the most junior member, that new colleague proved to be invaluable regarding our collaboration with the French team.

What happened? He spoke French. Even though the working language was English throughout the client organization, it had not become second nature to most staff. Thus, things got lost in translation and eventually made the situation more inconvenient for everyone involved. Speaking the same language opened doors. Moral of the story? Learn languages.

If you want to succeed in today's corporate world, an international mindset is vital. Cross-cultural competence, even if just obtained through backpacking parts of Asia, goes a long way. However, to be able to truly connect, there is no better way than speaking a common tongue. I am not suggesting that everyone should turn into a polyglot. Speaking dozens of foreign languages is great, but that by itself might not prove very useful for your career.

That being said, if you are working in an environment foreign to you, you should make an effort to obtain a certain competence in the local language. At the very minimum, you should be able to speak the language (even if just the basics) of the country where your company's headquarter is located or the language of other relevant markets.

For example, one of the people interviewed for this book speaks Spanish. That was not a reason why he got hired—because he is working in France. However, his limited competence in the Spanish language proved extremely valuable when some board member from the global headquarters (a Spaniard) came to visit. Who do you think that senior figure stayed in contact with even after his visit to France?

Likewise, if you know that in order to make it big in your company a stint in Indonesia is required, learning some Indonesian will not hurt. Basically, this will put you on the map in your company. Who do you think they would rather transfer abroad, the one who speaks some or none (such was the case for a long time in one of the largest fast-moving consumer goods companies in the world).

KEY TAKEAWAYS

♦ Acknowledge that continuous learning is not a buzzword. It is the very foundation to develop your skills and expertise, and ultimately what keeps you in business.

♦ Honestly assess your strengths and weaknesses. Identify what skills you can leverage by developing further and what areas of improvement need to be tackled the most.

♦ Use all available internal resources. There are plenty of opportunities for career starters to cultivate knowledge, including classroom and online trainings and knowledge-sharing platforms. It is up to you to make the most of these opportunities.

♦ Look elsewhere when internal resources are insufficient. Invest in books, online courses, and external courses to fill the identified learning gap. Try to secure funding from your company.

♦ Take personal responsibility for your learning. Don't limit yourself to a standard curriculum. Develop an excessive reading habit to continuously broaden your horizons.

♦ Become an idea machine. Challenge yourself creatively. Come up with ten ideas every day to keep your brain well exercised.

♦ Use foreign languages in your favor. Even though English has become the *lingua franca* in today's business world, connecting with people works best if you use their native language. Don't underestimate the importance of foreign languages to your career.

[11]

Networking Effectively

"People do business with people they know and like."

Keith Ferrazzi, *Never Eat Alone*

ETWORKING IS KEY IN most professions these days. "People who seem to 'have it all' have captured the hearts and conquered the minds of hundreds of others who helped boost them, rung by rung, to the top of whatever corporate of social ladder they chose," says relationship expert Leil Lowndes[42]. For those just starting out, establishing an internal network should be the first order of the day. No workday should be complete without nurturing existing relationships and bonding with people you have not met yet.

This topic is of vital importance. First, I will give you my general take on networking and how to network effectively. We will then conclude with an illustration of four often-overlooked groups of people that many people, especially juniors, do not have on their radar, and highlight the importance of networking with them (Figure 10).

A PRIMER ON NETWORKING

Networking is the process of building relationships with other people. All parties should benefit from the relationship in some form or other. Benefits can take on many different shapes, from lending support and giving advice to opening doors. Connecting with other people is particularly important for junior-level resources trying to make themselves known in an organization. After all, if no one knows you, who is going to consider you for anything to begin with? Besides, networking has been shown to have a direct effect on one's long-term salary growth rate too.[43] Thus, you need to establish your network early on.

To be sure, networking does not primarily serve as a vehicle to solve problems. Reaching out to other people when you need their help might work every once in a while, but this is not technically networking. This is simply asking for help. Networking should not occur when you need help from other people; it should happen well before that.

Successful networkers rely on connections that they have nurtured for a long time before ever asking for anything in return. Seek to establish a connection first, and determine what you can bring to the relationship. "To get value, give value ... If you're just starting out on your path, and you've got nothing else to give, then give your enthusiasm and your willingness to implement other people's advice," says career expert Ellsberg.[44] How can you add value? How can you make the other person's life a little easier?

And why should people network within their own company? Some of the main benefits for career starters include:

- **Getting things done:** First and foremost, you will have to get your own work done. Oftentimes, this necessitates input from other people. At a minimum, their collaboration could make things much easier. As a junior, however, you have no real say in an organization. Thus, other people's collaboration greatly depends on their goodwill. Developing trusting relationships can go a long way.

- **Sharing resources:** While most people have their specific job profiles, at times, you will find yourself in situations where you will depend on other people to give you a helping hand. Whether it is skills you do not have or simply capacity constraints, your network can come to the rescue and help turn things around when you cannot do so by yourself.

- **Receiving mental support:** Particularly during times of tribulation, which most of us will experience in one way or another, it pays to have a network one can rely on.

- **Increasing visibility:** Knowing people is one thing, while being known is another. If other people have you on their radar, they may consider you for future opportunities. Likewise, this increased visibility is bound to impact your reputation favorably.

- **Obtaining (confidential) information:** You cannot have your ears everywhere. Networking is one way to expand your reach within an organization by collaboratively sharing information. When done effectively, you can tap into advice and expertise, particularly from more experienced senior colleagues, that you wouldn't otherwise be able to access.

- **Broadening your network of connections:** When you engage in networking, you build potentially valuable connections, but it does not stop there. You do not only connect with your direct counterpart. In fact, you open yourself to a web of relationships that goes far beyond that. It's not just about who you are networking with directly, because that person will already have a network that you can (sooner or later) tap into.

- **Becoming more confident:** Some people are naturally reserved. A fresh start in an organization can be a welcome opportunity to do things a bit differently. Stepping out of your comfort zone to establish relationships beyond what is required to get work done can encourage even the more reserved among us to gain more confidence in expressing themselves and their perspectives.

Is this list comprehensive? No. But these points should be sufficient in making you actively engage in networking, even if you do not like the term, or if you think of yourself as too shy.

What Constitutes Effective Networking?

It is one thing to understand the importance of networking. It is something entirely different to actually act upon it. While there are potential pitfalls, networking certainly does not have to be a daunting exercise. Let's discuss how to network, what tools to use, where to network, and what to do in case there are limited networking opportunities.

How to Network

Follow the seven principles below to begin your networking activities on a solid foundation:

- **Be likeable:** You should always come across as a genuinely nice person. Having a certain degree of emotional intelligence goes a long way.[45] Be humble, and do not try to impress by being too eager. Leave that to others. If anything, try to impress in a natural, modest fashion.

- **Introduce yourself:** *Always* introduce yourself. If you meet someone you have not met yet, greet that person warmly. This is not just something to remember in your first weeks but should actually become your *modus operandi*. Regardless of whether people are more junior or senior to you, always connect. Understand who they are and where in the organization they fit. This also applies when you are working in an open-space office. You will frequently be surrounded by new faces, so don't become one of those guys who simply sneaks in and out, trying not to be seen. Trust me, they exist.

- **Be goal-oriented:** When you network, try to have at least a vague idea of what you want to get out of the relationship as well as what you could bring to it. This will help you use your networking time more effectively. Instead of talking for hours on end with people who will have no impact on your professional development (e.g., if they work in an entirely different part of the organization), you will know when to stop after getting their names and professions. Be aware of what you should be looking for. If you can learn something valuable from people in other parts of the organization, you should definitely tap into their knowledge. Some insights you gain from them or the connection itself might come in handy when you face future project challenges.

- **Reach out frequently:** Given the relatively high turnover in the industry, you want to keep track of your network. Don't let farewell emails sent to "Corporate All" take you by surprise. If you have to, schedule follow-ups with specific people in your calendar. This is what the best networkers do. They don't take chances; they put the right systems in place.

- **Follow up after first encounters:** We all meet a lot of people as we move through life. Often, we forget their names the minute after we have been introduced. Follow up the next day to stay on their minds.

- **Take specific time to network:** You can network all day long and then realize that you have not actually gotten much else done. Therefore, separate networking from formal working time.

- **Don't gossip:** Many people have an interest in the office trash, but you never know what you might be getting yourself into. Thus, don't waste your time gossiping. Besides, if you're talking about other people, what do you expect them to do when you're not around?

If some of this sounds familiar, then you've been reading carefully. These principles partly take into account the objectives discussed in Chapter 2. In short, what works when you first start by and large will serve you well for the rest of your career.

Tools to Enhance Your Networking Activities

The best networkers do not leave things to chance. They have adopted systems or processes that enable them to network effectively. The following tools and practices are not exclusive, but they do give you a flavor of what can work.

- **Calendar reminders (free):** One of the most effective practices is to regularly remind yourself to follow up with key people. In your calendar, you can schedule recurring events for a variety of reasons.

  – Calling your mentor (monthly)

- Networking with peers (quarterly)

- Reaching out to important groups of which you are a member (monthly/quarterly)

- Birthdays (annually)

- **Enhanced contacts in your email client (free):** The contact list in your email account can be further enhanced with additional information. You will have to do the work and enter the information yourself, but it might come in handy later.

- **Nextcall app (Android; free):** Nextcall keeps track of how frequently you call certain people. Even better, you can cluster your contacts and assign different call intervals for each. An automatic reminder will then alert you when it is time to call a certain contact.

- **Clinck app (iOS, Android; free):** Clinck allows you to easily share your contact details with people when you don't have your business cards handy.

- **Excel-based relationship tracking (free):** One of the easiest ways to track key contacts is to set up a simple Excel tracking tool. You don't have to create these from scratch; search online for "Excel CRM template" for free resources to utilize.

- **Evernote Business for Salesforce.com (paid):** While probably not required in your first two years, anyone working in a business driven by relationships should have Evernote Business on his or her radar. Salesforce.com is one of the most powerful customer relationship management (CRM) services. In combination with Evernote, the leading note-capturing application, these two form a powerful tool to deepen your professional relationships.

WHERE TO NETWORK

There are plenty of different networking opportunities available in most organizations. When looking for networking opportunities, consider the following (timeless) options:

- **Office:** The office is a great networking playground. Particularly in open-space environments, you will meet plenty of people. Take advantage of that. Connect with those you know and introduce yourself to those you have not met yet. Always keep your ears open. Refrain from checking out by putting on your headphones (even if you feel you are more productive with music). There may be exceptional circumstances that require you to block out other noise, but this is generally a pitfall to avoid.

- **Official events:** Chances are that there will be regular events for your company or respective department, and, depending on the size of the organization, even exclusive events for new hires. Attend those unless there is a very good reason not to.

- **Email:** Reach out to connect. Email is particularly useful for those irregular updates when you are not sharing the same office.

- **Unofficial events:** There are no limits here. This could range from informal gatherings with your colleagues at a bar or breakfast before work to lunch meetings and brunch on the weekends.

There are those people who distinguish strictly between work and private matters. Let me be clear, you are not supposed to become "friends" with your entire company. However, collaborative professional relationships will have to be nurtured just like personal relationships. They don't just happen; they require some effort. At the very least, regularly catching up over lunch or coffee is something you should consider.

What If There Are No Networking Opportunities?

There are *always* networking opportunities even though there are folks who claim that it was more difficult to build their networks than other professionals.

Typical Excuses

There may be situations that are less than ideal for working on your internal network. However, here is the good news: most of this is due to excuses from those who will not last long. They likely include the following:

- **I Don't Have Time:** Yes, there will be times during which you will have to juggle different pieces of work simultaneously. You might have to forego lunch and even cancel certain meetings. However, this can only be a short-term exception. Not having time is not an excuse on a regular basis. There is always time. For instance, for a short note to one's team to keep in touch or for a quick stop-by to see your colleagues for their after-work drinks.

- **It's Just Not Common Over Here:** Others claim that some environments are not right for networking. Opportunities to connect outside of your workplace may actually be quite rare. Perhaps it has just never been done before in a specific team. What does this tell you about your team? More importantly, what does this mean for you? Basically, you will have a great opportunity to stand out if you can set things in motion. Be a self-starter, because that is what is ultimately expected of you. No one will stop you from doing something worthwhile for the team.

HOW TO MAXIMIZE POOR NETWORKING OPPORTUNITIES

There are always ways to work around difficult situations. Use the following ideas as starting points to create networking opportunities and make yourself known.

- **Dial in to team calls (if applicable):** At some point, you might realize that the direct benefits are minimal, but early in your career, you have no reason not to join team calls. You would be surprised how many people never make an effort to attend. Eventually, these are the same guys who are unknown in the firm or practice, if they are known for anything at all (only slightly exaggerating here).

- **Schedule team drinks:** Talk to your boss and ask him or her if you could invite the team out for team drinks. Your boss will probably appreciate your initiative and make some of the budget available. These types of activities also tend to go a long way in performance ratings.

- **Send your team an update when abroad:** At times, you might end up on a project that is truly out of sight and possibly out of mind. Perhaps you are required to work on a client site all week. In such cases, meeting in person (and perhaps attending calls) may be a challenge. You should at least occasionally notify your team that you're still alive. Also, follow up with your team lead and managers one month before your scheduled project roll-off. Don't disappear from their radars. By sending a quick update, you will stand out despite being out of sight. As with anything, don't overdo it.

- **Share useful information with the team:** Apart from sending an update to your team (especially to senior leaders), you might want to consider sharing material or information that you deem relevant and useful to others. This could be anything, including new tools or the latest research in your field.

What else can you think of? Don't limit your options to these suggestions! So far, we have covered Networking 101. Now, let's take a closer look at how to network with specific people in your company. This is in addition to those stakeholders we discussed in Chapter 4. Here, we will elucidate important stakeholders that many people do not consider to be part of their network.

OFTEN-OVERLOOKED PEOPLE TO CONNECT WITH

All the networking advice in the world will only get you so far if you forget to see the bigger picture. Time and again, I have seen people struggle to build their networks because they were too narrowly focused. I was certainly not a natural-born networker myself. I had to learn a fair share in my early years too.

What some people never get right is looking beyond their team. Some are so focused on their immediate environment that they fail to see other important pieces of the jigsaw puzzle that can make or break their career progress. For simplicity's sake, let's call these people "gatekeepers." They are individuals who, on paper, may not play a crucial role in the organization but can stand in your way by their sole existence or open doors for you that you were completely unaware of.

Again, if you are working in a small company, it is very likely that not all of the below roles will apply to your situation. Organizations

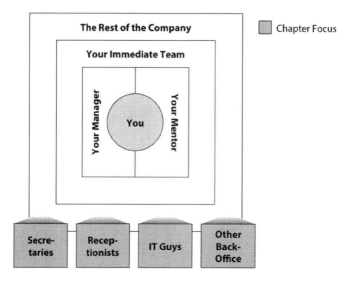

Figure 9: Networking Landscape (optional)

differ, after all. Nevertheless, the tasks performed by the four groups below are very common. Thus, even in small companies, someone will be responsible for these tasks and therefore will qualify as a valuable networking target.

What follows is a brief introduction of each of these four groups: secretaries, receptionists, IT guys, and other back-office support staff (also see Figure 9). For each group, we will discuss their relevance, their most common challenges, and ways to develop and maintain mutually beneficial relationships with them.

SECRETARIES

Secretaries are not always known by that name. Chances are, they will be called an "executive assistant" or something similar to that. That also indicates their current role. First and foremost, these individuals support a very senior person in the organization. Thus, do not expect them to be overly proactive in seeking to support you or other (senior) colleagues.

WHY THEY MATTER

Secretaries are the senior leaders' guardians. They are the primary gatekeeper between you and your boss. They manage the agenda and often perform an initial review of the inbox, distinguishing the important from the unimportant.

As a result, they are the ones who can squeeze you into a tight schedule. It might only be five minutes, but that's often all it takes to get a yes/no from your boss. Secretaries can open doors—or keep them shut.

THEIR CHALLENGES

Given the people they work for, their workload can often be intense. At times, people in other functions tend to forget this. Also, a lot of people will be asking for something from them. To be more precise, they want something *through* them, as those "secretaries" are standing in between ordinary employees and their boss.

For the most part, secretaries do a tremendous job without getting much back in return. They might get a bit of courtesy from the senior leaders, but that's about it. Moreover, there are often no clear career paths for them besides staying close to their senior leaders. This can be frustrating for those more junior in a secretarial role.

HOW TO KEEP THEM HAPPY

Obviously, as a junior-level resource, there is not much you can do about the work of secretaries and the challenges they face. However, you can give them some sincere attention when you're around. Don't only pass by when you need something or have a request. Be considerate and stop to have a genuine chat. Make them feel that you are part of the same team and respect them.

RECEPTIONISTS

Guess what? Receptionists do have their own place. It's called the reception. Not too surprising....

WHY THEY MATTER

Receptionists are important both at your office and on a client site. Granted, they primarily provide logistical support (e.g., making meeting rooms available, providing access to external visitors, calling taxis, etc.), but this role should not be understated. In your day-to-day activities, it will make a huge difference whether you have friendly support from the receptionists when you are in need or instead have to beg for their time. Make an effort to bond with receptionists.

THEIR CHALLENGES

Receptionists meet a lot of people on any given day, but how many of those actually make an effort to exchange more than a simple greeting? Keep in mind that they have barely any of the perks that ordinary employees may enjoy. Fancy dinners? Team events? Weekly company drinks? Receptionists are usually left out of the equation unless it is a firm-wide annual event.

In short, receptionists seldom receive the recognition they deserve. Time and again, juniors in particular make the mistake of perceiving and (even worse!) treating receptionists as colleagues of a lower rank. This might not be suicide for your career, but it can still have negative consequences.

HOW TO KEEP THEM HAPPY

To keep receptionists happy and build friendly relationships with them, stop doing what everyone else does. Instead, talk to them regularly and show some interest. Don't only interact with them when you have requests. Everyone does that, but you should know better.

IT GUYS

Your IT department takes care of all the technical equipment that you use on a daily basis, whether remotely or at the office. They regularly update, refurbish, restock, and resolve technical issues when necessary.

WHY THEY MATTER

One of the first groups you will probably meet early in your career are the guys in IT, either because they hand out your new devices or because something you need simply doesn't work. However, they will be instrumental to you far beyond your first days on the job.

Every now and then, you will experience hiccups with your technology. For example, you might have trouble connecting to a client's network due to security settings, or some specific piece of software will have to be bought for your project purposes. Whatever the situation may be, where your equipment is involved, your IT department will have to be consulted. It therefore pays to have (very) good relationships with them. Otherwise, you might be told to open a ticket and wait....

THEIR CHALLENGES

Just like many other back-office roles, the guys in IT suffer from a low level of recognition. For the most part, they are problem solvers (but few people actually thank them), and they are commonly scolded when their turnaround time is not quick enough.

HOW TO KEEP THEM HAPPY

IT guys are easy to please, given the low level of recognition they usually receive from the firm. A chat over coffee and showing genuine interest in how things are going for them will go a long way to establishing better (*read*: more personal) relationships than most people in other divisions have with IT professionals.

If you want to go above and beyond, do what successful senior people do and treat the IT guys to some considerate, but relatively effortless, courtesies during the holiday season (e.g., chocolates).

OTHER BACK-OFFICE SUPPORT STAFF

The back-office support staff includes professions like marketing, human resources, recruiting, finance, legal, or research. They differ from the previous four groups in that they are "optional" from a networking perspective. Their value can be significant if you engage them properly. However, if you do not, it will probably not impact your career negatively either. In contrast, you can hardly get anything done if you are not properly handling your networking with the first four groups.

WHY THEY MATTER

The benefits you can draw from these other support functions are manifold. However, at the core, their importance boils down to greater flexibility. If you have them on your side . . .

- Marketing can help you publish your study and even advise on how to secure funding

- HR may speed up the recruiting process with a candidate that you have preselected for your team

- Legal may provide counsel, despite being knee-deep in their own issues

- Finance may process certain invoices on your behalf or provide payment extensions

- Media & PR may open up their network and provide you with contacts you could not have personally secured

THEIR CHALLENGES

While a broad generalization, there is often a different pace in business units that function closer to the customer. Therefore, it does not go over well if you approach them with ad hoc requests that they could not have anticipated. Likewise, only showing up when you need something from them is not a good way to nurture the relationship. Due to this fact, support functions might not always come across as the most proactive.

Besides, by the very nature of their work, support functions are rarely involved in most of the "fun stuff" at work (e.g., celebrating successes). There might be firm-wide Christmas parties and summer events, but how often do they take place? Not often.

HOW TO KEEP THEM HAPPY

Given the relatively low level of recognition they receive on a daily basis, you don't have to move mountains in order to keep them happy. They appreciate feeling like a part of the wider firm, so go ahead and invite them to whatever firm-wide occasion you can think of. Informal after-work drinks don't need to be limited to members of your own team.

Besides, treat them like you would want others to treat you. You like to be greeted, so greet them. Don't miss the opportunity to briefly, casually connect with them when meeting in the hallway, elevator, or passing by their offices. Listen in on their views, worries, and suggestions. It will pay off handsomely if you can build sincere trusting relationships.

Having learned why and how to successfully connect with internal, often-overlooked stakeholders, let's look next in detail at one of the most important aspects of your career: the mentor–mentee relationship.

KEY TAKEAWAYS

♦ Build your network to advance your career. This cannot be accomplished overnight. It requires time and effort.

♦ Give first, take later. Invest in your relationships. Seek to provide value to your network before asking for anything in return.

♦ Be smart about networking. Put systems in place to regularly nurture relationships to simplify your efforts.

♦ Attend networking events. Do not forgo opportunities to connect with fellow colleagues. Initiate these opportunities if they're lacking in your company.

♦ Try to see the bigger picture. Network with those who are (often) left out. Engage in collaborative relationships with potential gatekeepers. This is an inexpensive way to really get things done, along with being the right thing to do.

[12]

Cultivating a Mentor Relationship

"He was always so zealous and honorable in fulfilling his compact with me, that he made me zealous and honorable in fulfilling mine with him."

Charles Dickens, *Great Expectations*

APART FROM HAVING A strong and supportive network, career starters should expend a great deal of effort in cultivating a trusting mentor relationship. In so doing, this may go well beyond the immediate corporate environment. This chapter will provide a deep dive into the peculiarities of mentors and mentees.

First, we shall consider why mentors of any type are important. Afterwards, we will split the discussion into two parts by discussing the dos and don'ts in terms of being a mentee within your company and to an external mentor, respectively. We will then conclude with some pointers about how to actually connect with a mentor.

WHY MENTORS MATTER

You cannot achieve much without the help of others. This has always been true. If you look at the majority of famous figures, you will recognize that they all had someone who guided them. Every successful person, regardless of what industry, has had a mentor (or a coach). Steve Jobs, Andy Grove. Eric Schmidt, Bill Campbell. Bill Gates, Warren Buffett. Satya Nadella, Bill Gates. Jack Dorsey, Bob Iger...the list goes on and on.

Mentors are very important. They can make the difference between getting ahead in your career and staying put. According to success expert Robert Greene, "Mentors do not give you a shortcut, but they streamline the process ... What took you ten years on your own could have been done in five with proper direction."[46] Mentors can give you perspective. And that is what most people struggle with: seeing themselves as others see them. Mentors can simply watch what you are doing and ask, "Is that what you really meant?" Over time, this will allow you to eliminate weaknesses as well as reduce mistakes.

Mentors can lend support in a multitude of other ways. From advising based on their own personal experience to leveraging their vast network of relationships, any career starter would be ill-advised to not seek out mentorship. In short, a mentor's hindsight can become a junior's foresight.

In the following section, we will first focus on mentors within your company, because that person will be the most relevant for you in the beginning. However, it is also good practice to have a trusted advisor outside your organization.

INTERNAL MENTORS OR COACHES

Many companies have recognized the importance of developing talent internally. As such, corporate mentoring programs are the norm, rather than the exception. It is this system that we refer to as having an internal mentor. As a rule of thumb, there still appears to be a divide between larger and smaller organizations, with the former usually having more formalized systems in place than the latter. However, the specific characteristics can differ sharply. In many organizations, career starters are assigned to a mentor, while others may be able to choose from a pre-selected pool of potential mentor candidates (this is more common in graduate trainee programs). Whatever situation you find yourself in—even if there are no formalized mentoring programs—you should make an effort to cultivate a strong mentor-mentee relationship within your company. The remainder of this chapter will show you how to go about doing that.

Your mentor is your guide in all career-related matters. Mind you, your mentor is not supposed to be your friend, as it is primarily a professional relationship. If the two of you can build a friendly, trusting relationship, that's even better. This can be a match made in heaven or turn out to be a complete disaster. To help you determine which situation you're in, I will provide a number of perspectives. First, we will put ourselves into the shoes of your mentor. We will then look at what the profile of a good internal mentor should look like and what to do in case you wish to change your internal mentor. Finally, I will provide you with some steps to take in case your company does not have a formalized mentoring program.

From the Perspective of the Internal Mentor

Your mentor will usually be a senior colleague, and he or she will have his or her own daily business challenges just like you. Thus, the mentor role is in addition to their usual workload and is not necessarily a top priority—even though that's what it should be (at least, in the case of formalized mentoring programs).

Keep in mind, your mentor probably didn't pick you out of the vast pool of high-caliber junior-level resources. More often than not, mentees are assigned based on a set of criteria, including:

- Which team do you belong to (mentors and mentees should not be aligned organizationally)?

- How many levels are between you and the mentor?

- Has your mentor played this role before?

- How many mentees does your mentor already have? It is not uncommon for mentors to have multiple mentees, although there are limits.

As a result, your mentor will have to start from scratch in terms of getting to know you. They will likely give you the benefit of the doubt, but this does not mean that you will get away with much. Your mentor will usually have a good understanding of what is required to excel in the industry in general and your company in particular. He or she will do his or her best to lead you in the right direction.

Provided that you buy in to the guidance offered, both of you will have a positive, relatively easy time. You will become like a tag team, furthering each other's careers as you go. If you do not wish to consider your mentor's advice, this relationship will not be fun for either of you, and it would be best to change your mentor quickly.

In order to make this relationship function as smoothly as possible, you will be expected to keep your mentor aware of your development. Seek his or her counsel for everything that is work- or career-related. That being said, your actions may not necessarily need to stop there.

In order to cultivate this relationship, your mentor will reach out to you from time to time (good mentors do this more often). But don't wait for it. In fact, if you have to be asked for an update, then you have probably been a little out of touch. Don't let this happen.

Instead, make it a habit to touch base with your mentor regularly, ideally in person or over the phone.

Unlike other colleagues, your mentor will hardly ever work directly with you. Thus, he or she will likely form an opinion based on feedback from other people and yourself. Therefore, the best way to build a trusting mentor-mentee relationship is to provide regular updates. Regard your mentor as your guardian or wingman. He or she is there to help, provided that you trust each other. That trust is built over time by sharing whatever you have on your mind and being open to feedback.

What Is a Good Internal Mentor?

The profile of a good internal mentor is quite straightforward. Obviously, character traits are different, and what appeals to me might not appeal to you. The mentor–mentee relationship is very personal, so you should ensure that you click with the person giving you career advice and guidance. Nevertheless, there are certain competencies that a good internal mentor should have to be truly valuable in your career progression:

- Minimum four years of experience with the firm

- Started off as a junior in the company (i.e., knows exactly what the challenges for juniors are)

- Was promoted according to plan or faster (i.e., knows how to get ahead)

- Willing to give honest feedback

- Sports an extensive internal network, which may be leveraged for a mentee's cause

- Diligently performs mentoring duties by making time available, when need be, and holding mentees accountable

Some of the above pointers can only be determined through first-hand experience and are difficult to ascertain beforehand, so it is a bit of a gamble, but all of the above is informed by my very positive mentee experience (hat tip to Marco Issenmann and Felix Hauber) as well as the less than ideal experiences of some colleagues of mine. As such, I encourage you to seek mentorship from those who closely match these aspects.

WHAT TO DO IF YOU WANT TO CHANGE YOUR OFFICIAL INTERNAL MENTOR

At times, you and your internal mentor might not be a perfect match. Perhaps your mentor is simply not as invested in his or her mentoring role. In that case, there are always ways to change and find a new one. If the relationship is not an official one, then there is not much to worry about. Find a new one. However, if this relationship is an official arrangement, you have to proceed more carefully. Here are the four steps that have worked for others.

1. **Do not speak to your mentor immediately:** Those more senior to you usually have more experience and boast a wider network in the organization. Therefore, you want to proceed strategically (carefully). You want to avoid ruining your relationship with your mentor and potentially shutting alternative doors from the start.

2. **Understand the official process:** Contact HR or ask fellow colleagues you trust about how the process of changing one's mentor typically works in your company.

3. **Identify a potential new mentor:** Identify a potential mentor, and ask if he or she would be available and willing to take you on as a new mentee in the future. You do not have to be overly specific about your current mentor or the fact that you are considering making a change.

Keep it informal and say that you think your career might benefit from a fresh perspective.

4. **Follow the official process:** Once you have found someone who generally agrees to mentor you, have a word with your existing mentor. Let him or her know that you plan to proceed with the next official steps.

To summarize, it's essential to have a great relationship with your mentor. As such, I recommend that you first make an effort to improve the relationship in case it is not working to your satisfaction. Only after you have tried to improve it (and have spoken with your mentor on how to turn things around) should you go ahead and seek alternatives.

WHAT TO DO IF THERE IS NO MENTORING PROGRAM

Chances are good that there is no official mentoring program in your company whatsoever. This is not a great start, but there is no need to despair either. For many of the people who were interviewed for this book, the relationship to the person they perceived as their true mentor has never actually been formalized. In fact, serendipity is not uncommon. The relationship has simply grown over time. What may start as a simple catch-up over coffee once in a while might turn into a regular session of career-related counsel.

Ultimately, everyone just starting out needs someone supportive in their early years, especially if an individual is new to the industry, if only to provide reassurance in times of doubt. This someone does not have to come with a "mentor" label or even be aligned to you organizationally. Often it is helpful if you and your mentor are not working closely on a day-to-day basis, as it allows for a more unbiased, objective perspective.

However, this person should be willing to take you under their wing, because mentoring cannot be a one-way street. The other party—the mentor-to-be—also must be willing to serve as a mentor to you. Now, simply waiting for the relationship to turn into a proper mentor-mentee relationship is something that may work, but I suggest you do the following:

1. Identify a potential mentor candidate (ideally based on the criteria discussed above)

2. Seek out opportunities to work together, support, or mingle with that person

3. Once some relationship has been established (which takes time and should not occur until you have been with the company for two months or more), ask if that person would be willing to provide you with more regular guidance and coaching (avoid the term mentoring, because this sounds like work).

EXTERNAL MENTORS

Here is some good news if your company does not have an official mentoring program and none of your colleagues seem like an ideal mentor candidate—internal mentors are not the only source of guidance. In fact, everyone should have an external mentor in addition to the one assigned by one's firm.[47]

An external mentor can benefit your development in ways that an internal mentor often cannot. For starters, an external mentor is objective. Clearly, someone outside the firm does not have any say in your career progression within the firm, and that is also the biggest advantage. He or she is not related to your firm and can provide you with a perspective that internal colleagues cannot. In addition, you can freely share your concerns and career aspirations (which may go beyond your firm) without worrying about negative consequences.

There is not a single best approach for finding an external mentor. One thing is certain; you'll have to invest both effort and time. You can't find a mentor overnight. To get you thinking, start considering any of the following people to act as a future external mentor:

- A university professor you have always admired or who has been instrumental in furthering your career

- A relative you respect for his or her business acumen

- Someone in your local community who has had ten to twenty years of experience in his or her field

Focus on people who have enjoyed success in some form or other and whose advice you genuinely respect. If none of the above apply to someone in your network, then simply go with the next best person in your circle of friends. Is a somewhat successful friend five years or more ahead of you in his or her career? Seek out guidance from that person. Don't get stuck by looking for that perfect mentor.

How to Connect with Your Mentor

Becoming a good mentee to your mentor cannot be learned by reading a book or following some cookie-cutter business advice.[48] It takes effort and time. Whether you have an internal or external mentor, or both, you should seek to create a mutually beneficial relationship. As such, this should not be a one-way exchange of ideas and rewards. Your mentor invests time in your development, so you should reciprocate in some form or other. To enhance the relationship do the following.

- **Provide frequent updates:** Your mentor should always have a clear idea about your current situation. This does not mean you have to report weekly but catching up once a month (or quarterly at the very least) helps keep your mentor in the loop. You should also inform him or her as soon as you encounter challenges that may have an impact on your professional development. Critical turning points should not take your mentor by surprise.

- **Acknowledge feedback:** You do not have to agree with all the feedback you receive, but you have to be open and receptive. It is good practice to thoroughly consider certain advice and inform your mentor on specific steps taken and progress made.

- **Show gratitude:** A simple thank you never hurts, but that's probably not enough to build a truly great relationship. Instead, express your gratitude by taking your mentor out for lunch or dinner, buy him or her a bottle of wine, or simply write him or her a little thank you note.

Key Takeaways

- Have a mentor. As examples of successful business leaders show, a more experienced person can be instrumental in your personal and professional development.

- Leverage mentoring options within your company. Whether formally or informally arranged, career starters can benefit greatly from someone's guidance in settling into a new organization and industry.

- Don't be afraid to change mentors, if necessary. Relationships evolve. If you feel that some official mentor is not the right fit, take action and look elsewhere.

- Look beyond your corporate boundaries for mentorship. Consider finding an external mentor to benefit from even more objective, unbiased council.

♦ Invest in the relationship. Building a strong mentor–mentee relationship takes time and effort. Taking their advice to heart and being open to feedback are the first crucial steps.

[13]

Beyond Business-As-Usual

"If someone offers you an amazing opportunity and you're not sure you can do it, say yes—then learn how to do it later."

Sir Richard Branson

ONE OF THE CORE premises of this book is that business-as-usual is not enough to start a successful career. If you follow your job description to the letter, you will be mediocre at best. The good news is eventually you will have the opportunity to work on areas that are not part of your day-to-day job. "While it's good to be directed in your career, you'll want to stay open and alert to unexpected possibilities. And when they show up, act on them. You never know what the outcome might be," says Jocelyn Glei, writer about work- and career-related matters.[49] Instead of trying to steer clear from those extra jobs, you should embrace them.

We will split this chapter into three parts. First, we will shed some light on the meaning of your job description. We will then continue by discussing special internal projects and consulting projects. You will learn what they are all about and why you should be an active member of both, if possible. Particularly for consulting projects, I will draw from my own consulting experience to help you understand why they matter, how to work with consultants best when you are the client, and how you can leverage the relationship for your own personal needs.

YOU ARE NOT YOUR JOB DESCRIPTION

When you are just starting out, you will likely be assigned a set of tasks and objectives. Your role means that you are expected to perform a fixed set of activities, but keep in mind that companies and their very teams may differ. You might be expected to be up and running very quickly, or you may be handed a "lighter" version of your role to fulfill in the beginning. Either way, do not expect that what everyone asks you for is the only thing you should be aiming to achieve.

Aim to tick all the boxes quickly. Make sure you do exactly what is expected of you based on specific requests, as well as your official job profile. Unless mediocrity is your objective, do not stop there. You should develop what Simon Hartley calls "'relentless inquisitiveness', the drive to learn more and be better."[50] Go above and beyond. Raise your hand and volunteer. Show you are a quick learner and hungry for more. Show your willingness to collaborate. Get to know people. Learn new stuff. Perhaps develop your first little niche in the staff. Show that you are not only good at what you have been hired for. Build your reputation. The earlier you can do this—and perhaps deliver something that you can showcase later on as you go—the better.

Likewise, if someone asks you to work on something that you feel unqualified for, do not panic. Do it anyway. Give it a try. If that person did not think you could manage it, you wouldn't have been considered to begin with.

INTERNAL PROJECTS, OR EXTRACURRICULAR ACTIVITIES IN THE BUSINESS WORLD

Think back to your time in college. Chances are, you got involved in some type of student association. That extracurricular work is what you prominently put on your CV later. In your professional career, the situation is quite similar.

There will be opportunities to shine in areas that are not necessarily related to your core job profile. Such opportunities range from organizing typical corporate events, such as a summer or Christmas party, or heading up certain specific initiatives, such as an employee feedback survey or innovation initiatives. These are all good opportunities to stand out. Some even offer very senior-level exposure (which you should seek early in your career). If you do a good job, you will likely experience positive spillover effects into your actual professional career. Thus, you should actively chase such opportunities, provided you can make a rational case for it. It is important to be proactive here because you might otherwise be assigned to a random piece of work by more senior people. It is not uncommon that extra work is expected. Choose yourself, instead. It will most likely work out in your favor.

CONSULTANTS AND OTHER PROFESSIONAL SERVICES

In addition to the above, there will be special projects within most larger organizations. This is often when external consultants are involved. Now, you might wonder why consultants should really matter to you. After all, you have a clearly defined job description, but you will most likely come across them sooner or later in your career.

By and large, there are two ways in which you might potentially engage with consultants at work. First, you might be assigned to a project team based on your role within the organization. For example, if consultants are helping to optimize a certain operational process in the value chain and you happen to be a part of the supply chain team, you might end up in that very project. Second, you might not be a member of a project team but still be involved in some form or other, such as by providing information or expertise on an ad hoc basis.

WHY CONSULTANTS ARE HIRED

Unfortunately, some people have knee-jerk reactions when they hear anything about consulting. This can also be the case in companies that opt for hiring a consultant team. For various reasons, consultants expect to be met with a certain degree of distance, if not mistrust, when they start a new project. Often this is simply based on poor communication within the client organization prior to the project kick-off. People are simply not sure about the purpose of the consulting engagement and naturally get a little uneasy. However, it does not have to be that way, and, quite frankly, most of these concerns are unfounded.

Why do companies hire consulting firms? Because they have a need they want to address. In other words, consultants fill a gap that someone in the client organization realized could not be filled in any other way. Conceptually, all of these needs fall into one of three categories: resources, mandate, and expertise.

RESOURCES

A company might have the right competencies and know what to do but simultaneously lack the resources to execute certain initiatives. Employees usually fulfill clearly defined roles. Therefore, shifting resources without risking the structure and functionality of the entire company is a challenge. You can assign people to some new internal project, but what about the existing tasks? Eventually, one or the other has to give. Thus, companies are often faced with a simple resource issue. They could hire staff members to fill the gap, but will they find the right candidate quickly? How long will the onboarding process take? What do you do with the resource once the task has been accomplished?

MANDATE

A company may also hire consultants to execute initiatives. Someone internal might know what should happen, but they either lack the experience and knowledge to get it done or feel that third parties, when properly mandated, are in a better position to break through potential internal resistance. A corporate employee might be able to accomplish the same task, but this person might be "burned" in the process, at which point his or her future in the company is limited. What is required is not just the ability to get the job done but also the political savvy and ability to garner organizational support. All of this comes with experience and, above all, independence.

EXPERTISE

At other times, companies simply do not know what to do. This is the third classic case where consultants can be of help. What external service providers can contribute, in contrast to most internal resources, is typically much broader industry experience, greater exposure to different corporate challenges, and experience in finding solutions to such problems, as well as extensive expertise in best practices (including technology, processes, or others).

In short, companies engage consulting firms to help them by providing temporary highly skilled labor, innovative solutions, and deep industry expertise. Contrary to what some people may inherently feel, you should welcome the arrival of external consultants because they are there to help. They want to provide real tangible value, since that is the only way to generate repeat business. As such, they can and want to be your partner.

How to Work with Consultants

In order to optimize your experience when working with consultants, it helps to understand their needs and ways of working. Consultants usually work on very tight deadlines. This is not necessarily self-imposed but is simply the nature of the service provided. Clients rightly expect the speedy delivery of results.

In a typical consulting project, the consultants will try to get up to speed quickly. To that end, they need to understand the peculiarities of their clients. Let me be clear, consultants will come prepared. Colleagues who have worked with the company before have likely briefed the new consultants. The so-called lead client service partner, who manages the relationship between the consulting firm and the client company, will have ensured that all consultants are fully prepared. This may involve informational briefings before the project kick-off or even entire training programs concerning the client business. Furthermore, successful consultants also take responsibility in terms of getting up to speed by reading anything from the company's annual reports, press releases and investor material to product catalogues and industry reports.

However, once the project begins, consultants usually require additional information, particularly as projects evolve. The type of information depends on the project obviously, but broadly speaking, they often need either more factual information or specific insights.

Factual information is all about specific data points required to get the job done. Depending on the project, these may be financial metrics or process plans. Some of this will have been required (and provided by the client company) from the start. Often, it only becomes clear after a few days, through additional conversations with the client or upon receiving (potentially poor) information, that additional input is needed.[51] This is usually when consultants need to reach out to experts in the client organization. Help them if you can (and have the authority to do so). Do not try to play hard ball, because ultimately, it is you (through one of your bosses) who will pay for results from the consultants. Given that, you might as well help to make it a smooth process for everyone involved.

The second type of input consultants need is insights specific to your company or specific project. Remember, not all information is codified and can be handed over. While they have often seen other organizations face similar challenges to those they are helping to solve in your company, consultants often rely on you and your other colleagues to provide a company-specific perspective. Therefore, feel free to provide your view. For you, personally, there is no risk of over-sharing really. Challenge the consultants if you have a reason to. Do not feel intimidated. They typically appreciate open exchange with client personnel, as this is what ultimately helps them achieve long-term results.

You will probably only occasionally work with consultants, and, if so, it will be a single piece of a larger puzzle. It is very unlikely that you will have to manage a consultant team or act as the sole point of contact. In the unlikely event that you do have to step up, focus on the following aspects to increase your odds of getting consulting projects right:

- Agree on the project scope (what is included and what is not)

- Clarify expectations regarding project deliverables

- Coordinate ways of working, i.e., communicate how you would like to work (but remain somewhat adaptive if need be) and understand the consultant team's style of work (within reason)

- Maintain frequent interaction with consultants (check points)

- Encourage consultants to go deeper in their analyses (if applicable)

- Connect consultants with people vital to the project's success

- Learn to be uncomfortable, if necessary

How to Leverage the Relationship and Why

Similar to what I refer to as extracurricular activities, you should treat the relationship with consultants as an investment. As a career starter, there are many ways in which you can benefit from trusting consultant relationships, even if that project is only a one-off endeavor.

- **Get insights:** Consultants tend to be well informed and well organized, or at least they should be. Also, they like to help, so you may get insights into your own company that you would not have had otherwise. This does not come from me, but was actually a repeated theme in the interviews conducted for this book.

- **Learn new skills:** You might also be able to learn a thing or two from external consultants. Their areas of expertise can range from technical skills, such as financial modeling and time management, to more social soft skills, such as how to communicate effectively or work within an organization.

- **Prepare a potential career move:** While most consultancies are not actively recruiting from existing clients, you should not dismiss the potential opportunity of joining a consulting firm yourself. You never know how things are going to play out in the long run. Keep your options open.

- **Improve your (future) hiring:** Although this may still be a few years out, you might be looking for additional talent for your own team at some point. Consultants usually have a vast network, as well as colleagues who might be keen on joining another industry. Both may be leveraged, provided that you have built and maintained a relationship with your consultants. Even if you are a junior-level resource now, do not forget to lay the foundation for tomorrow's success today.

KEY TAKEAWAYS

◆ Follow your job description—and then over-deliver. Make sure you meet all objectives that are set for your specific role, but seek out gradually doing more than is expected.

◆ Support internal initiatives. Even if unrelated to your work, consider helping organize "stuff" for your company. Do not consider any task too mundane. Instead, focus on building a good company-wide reputation.

◆ Help your consultant out. Do not freeze when consultants ask for your input. Understand that you are likely sitting in the same boat, so you might as well help to make this a pleasant experience for everyone.

◆ Leverage the consulting experience. Trusting relationships with consultants can benefit you directly in multiple ways, both right now and in the future.

[14]

On Performance Management and Promotions

"Don't mistake activity with achievement."

John Wooden

HAVE YOU HEARD ABOUT Fortune 500 companies abandoning employee ratings? Well, this is newsworthy only because it remains an exception, and more often than not is just a pilot phase. For the most part, larger organizations continue to rely on employee performance evaluations. Some industries may be more feedback-driven than others, but regular assessments of your work can be expected.

This chapter sheds light on the most pressing issues when faced with performance management from the perspective of a junior just starting out. It is also informed by experiencing firsthand how many people are unable to accept constructive feedback—even though they should.

We will first look at why performance management matters. Second, we shall discuss the steps in a typical performance year. Finally,

I will provide some pointers about mitigating some of the most common challenges and how to receive feedback in the best way possible.

WHY PERFORMANCE MANAGEMENT MATTERS

Performance management is crucial in most large organizations. However, despite its importance, it is usually far from perfect. You will probably experience situations that seem unfair. Effort that you make might not always translate directly into equal rewards. In fact, most people feel that they never get offered a raise or promoted quickly enough. That's just the way it is.

However, given that you've made it this far in the book, you're likely one of those people who most industries are always looking for: ambitious, motivated, willing to learn, and possessed of personal drive. Therefore, you should not be overly concerned about performance management; in fact, you'll probably appreciate the process, provided you take charge.

HELPING YOU DEVELOP YOURSELF

First and foremost, performance management will help you in your own development by holding you accountable and pointing you toward areas to focus on in the future. At the beginning of each performance year, you will define certain objectives. These are focal areas that you want to pay attention to during the upcoming performance cycle. While you are being observed in the context of your current level's expectations, objectives can be rather personal. Depending on your strengths, weaknesses, and motivation, you will agree with your mentor (or your manager) on which things to focus on and what "success" at the end of the year would look like.

Performance discussions at the end of the year will then be used to measure your progression against your objectives. Your final rating and accompanying feedback will form the foundation in defining your new objectives for the following performance cycle. Thus, performance management can be a vital and ongoing system that helps you address weak points and become measurably better over time. However, you have to have absolute certainty from the beginning as to what grade-specific key performance indicators (KPIs) you are going to be rated against, especially since they may change from one year to another.

When I started out, Excel-based analytical skills were one of my development areas. I could get by, but like many others, I would not have regarded myself as "above average" either. As a result, one of my key objectives remained "enhancing Excel-based analytical skills" for a number of years. Therefore, I sought out opportunities (consulting projects, business development, and internal research activities) that would allow me to test the waters a bit more. Also, the feedback I requested was always related to my analytical performance.

CLEARING OUT THE BAD GUYS

Effective performance management can also be a useful tool to identify low performers in the organization. First, it will allow the firm to put those who are currently struggling on a new track. Specific feedback and an action plan for low performers can turn them around to become more valuable assets for the company. After all, training someone new all over again is much more time-consuming and costs more money (costs in excess of 10 times the cost of training)[52] than nudging someone back on track.

If all of this fails, obviously performance management should not refrain from dismissing low performers. This is in the best interest of the company and each employee working with the low performer, as the morale of others will fall when they realize that slack in the system is not being dealt with.

The Importance of Good Performance

Ultimately, any corporate performance management system is trying to evaluate how the employees have fared against relevant objectives. These objectives can differ. In fact, they change over the course of one's career. The importance of actual work does not appear to be constant; it changes with time and seniority.

In the beginning, all that matters is whether you are getting the job done. This usually entails very concrete, specific tasks. On top of that, it is also assumed that junior-level resources get along with their colleagues (i.e., being a team player). Over time, other factors gain importance. That does not mean that delivering tangible results at work does not matter any longer. However, the specific targets may change. For example, sales targets may replace utilization targets (i.e., the ratio of hours chargeable to customers vs. non-chargeable), but most importantly, you will see that there is an inverse relationship between the weight of merit and political savviness (see Figure 10).

For you, this means the merit trumps political savviness when you are just starting out. The actual work you deliver is paramount. Enhancing your political savviness is reflected in how well you leverage your network. Over time, you might experience a shift where your work output matters less, and your ability to "work the system" matters more.

For career starters, quality work can be sufficient in getting ahead to some degree, but more senior people will realize that work output alone will not be enough. Being able to build and leverage trusting relationships within the organization becomes significantly more crucial with increasing seniority. For now, focus on delivering high-quality work, and make sure it is assessed by your manager appropriately.

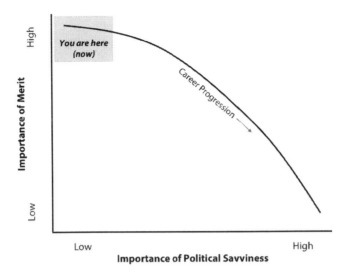

Figure 10: Merit vs. Political Savviness

THE PERFORMANCE MANAGEMENT PROCESS

The very structure of the performance management process differs between companies. Some companies conduct performance ratings annually or biannually. For some, this is done across the entire organization, while for others, it is managed within teams, e.g., business units or functions.

Regardless of what mechanism is applied in your company, you should consider the following performance management process as a reference for your own benefit. This is particularly important if your company does not follow a formal evaluation process, in which case, you should take matters into your own hands. Get in the driver's seat and set the agenda for your own career development.

For the sake of explanation, let's assume that we're dealing with an annual performance management process conducted throughout the entire organization that will look as follows (see Figure 11).

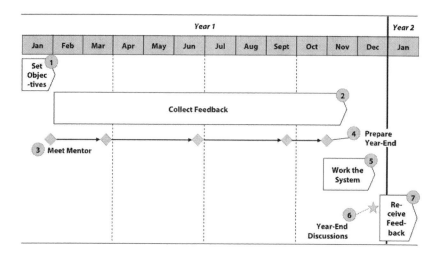

Figure 11: Sample Performance Management Process

1. **Months 0-1, define performance objectives:** At the be-ginning of each performance year, which may or may not coincide with the financial year, set your objectives. Usu-ally, they should be in line with the SMART[53] criteria and ultimately agreed upon by your mentor (or manager).

2. **Months 1-11, deliver exceptional work and collect feed-back (ongoing):** Throughout the year, you should collect feedback on your work. The key here is to request specif-ic feedback that can somehow be tied back to your orig-inal performance objectives. Feedback providers can be anyone you have worked with, including external parties (if applicable).

3. **Months 1-11, maintain regular catch-ups with your men-tor:** Throughout the performance year, you should stay in contact with your internal mentor. This process does not have to be overly formal. If there is a corporate per-formance management tool to capture and communi-

cate your progress, this should certainly be used. However, make sure you also have in-person opportunities to connect and discuss your development in terms of your annual objectives at least once every quarter. If you do not have a mentor in your company, then have these conversations with your manager.

4. **Month 11, prepare year-end discussion:** In some organizations, your mentor will have to represent you in final year-end discussions (sometimes called a "roundtable"). However, this is not the norm. It is widely considered the worst case, as it means more work for everyone involved. To set yourself up for success, you should provide your mentor with a concise, firsthand account of your performance so that he or she can represent you best in front of the company's senior leadership (see Point 6). Chances are, you will agree on a short action plan, including requesting outstanding feedback and confirmations, completing certain mandatory trainings, and ticking other boxes that your company may require (e.g., legal obligations, holiday take-over approval).

    In case your company does not have a solid performance management process in place, you should still have a final year-end discussion with your mentor (or manager) before being evaluated. This will not only allow you to clarify things but will also convey an attitude of taking responsibility and a willingness to prepare for your future career development.

5. **Months 11-12, work the system:** If performance evaluations are conducted company-wide with rigid benchmarks across the workforce, you and your mentor will have to lay a proper foundation beforehand. As such, you

206 | *Got the Job... Now What?*

should execute the plan on which you both agreed upon before the evaluation (see Point 4). This means that your mentor works his or her network and reaches out to key people whose support is needed during performance rating discussions. Here, you may think of those (senior) people with whom you worked during the performance year as well as your manager, and, at times and where applicable, even external parties. This will serve to garner support and validate specific feedback while also helping to mitigate certain risks (e.g., when you have received poor feedback).

Meanwhile, you will complete all open items that you and your mentor identified earlier (e.g., collecting feedback and complying with company-wide requirements). In addition, you might want to draft a one- or two-page overview of your performance as a cheat sheet for your mentor. This typically includes an overview of the core tasks performed, projects worked on, key feedback, trainings attended, other activities (including vacations, if any), and any other metrics that matter in your field (e.g., sales targets, customer satisfaction ratings, the ratio of chargeable vs. non-chargeable work). Be aware that reaching out to key people just prior to year-end discussions can backfire. You and your mentor should maintain relationships with those individuals that have a say in your development throughout the year.

6. **Month 12, discuss performance and agree on final ratings:** The very process of determining a rating of your performance is company-specific. In case you are evaluated solely by your manager (and within the realm of

your team), you are lucky. There is no additional work for you here.

In a full-blown company-wide evaluation process, your mentor will likely present on your behalf. These sessions are typically held separately for each level. Usually, the objective is to squeeze the range of employees into a bell curve. Thus, there can only be a handful of overachievers. The vast majority will be rated at a similar level. Each employee will be represented by his or her mentor (often for less than two minutes). This brief presentation should conclude with a rating suggestion to the panel. This is best accomplished when other colleagues have already been discussed, as your mentor will be able to put things (and your particular case) into context. Your mentor should not be the first to speak, regardless of how busy he or she may be that day. Otherwise, you will end up as the benchmark, and, through a process similar to horse-trading, slowly see your rating drop over the course of the session.

7. **Month 12+, receive rating and feedback, and conclude performance year:** Just before the start of the new performance year, you will receive your year-end rating and corresponding feedback. Depending on the depth of the latter, this might directly affect the new objectives you set for yourself. Also, whether your rating will coincide with a bonus payment or promotions is very case-specific. At the very minimum, you should understand what it will take to get to the next level based on your previous performance and corresponding evaluation.

PERFORMANCE MANAGEMENT CHALLENGES

Now, let me share a more personal view. The reason I had for writing this guide was not to provide a generic overview that you could have gotten from your HR department. Instead, this chapter, like the rest of the book, is intended to help you understand how things usually work and teach you specific steps to navigate the world of work in the best way possible.

A chapter on performance management would not be complete without addressing some of the recurring criticisms and potential remedies. By and large, the key reason for people criticizing performance ratings is due to their lack of transparency. Regardless of what more senior people might say, the process is usually not very transparent. Knowing how the process works is not the same as having insight into the actual dealings and understanding what has been negotiated in year-end discussions (or what your boss' rationale might have been). This is where most of the criticism stems from. Ratings and the rationale behind them are usually not publicly announced, which leaves room for speculation. In addition, in many industries, people complain about a lack of clarity in terms of promotion requirements. What does it take to get promoted? What skills do I have to develop? How long do I have to perform a certain role until being considered for higher levels?

One frequent perception is that ratings are not fair, slightly biased, and highly dependent on having viable connections within the corporate network. In my opinion, the only way to address such criticism is to provide full openness. At the very least, ratings and corresponding feedback should be visible for each and every employee. However, I am realistic enough to know that such changes are unlikely to be made in most organizations, so consider the following criteria that potentially affect your year-end rating, and work to improve them going forward.

YOUR QUALITY OF WORK

THE PROBLEM

I am convinced that the most important criterion for your rating remains the quality of your work. If you do a good job, then you will be off to a good start in the performance evaluation. However, keep in mind, doing a good job is expected. Delivering on expectations usually does not get you very far. On the other hand, if you fail to deliver, this will hit you hard.

THE REMEDY

In order to truly stand out, your work has to be exceptional. Not once, but *consistently*. Certain pieces of work tend to stand out more than others, so you will need to be somewhat selective in what jobs you pick up or what you even volunteer for. Thus, seek out great opportunities to learn from, continuously strive to become better, and consistently deliver high-quality work.

YOUR VISIBILITY

THE PROBLEM

Apart from good work, you will have to ensure that people know you. You should have some type of positive reputation, and people should immediately know who is being talked about when they hear your name. This is particularly important if you happen to be working remotely, which makes establishing/maintaining an office presence difficult, or if you are more engaged with external clients or parties other than your immediate team.

THE REMEDY

Do not assume that people will get to know you somehow. People won't know you unless you take matters into your own hands. Visibility is something that should be dealt with from Day 1, as it takes time to establish. This is also the reason why networking, as stressed in Chapter 11, is key. The best way to enhance your visibility is to volunteer for high-profile tasks and achieve them with exceptional quality. Such tasks include all those whose outcomes are widely shared within the company (or your particular part of it) and should ideally come with personal acknowledgement.

Moreover, in everything you do, be your own marketer. No one will provide free publicity for you. You have to take care of it yourself. If you don't, you're missing out. Research shows that actual performance doesn't always matter as much as being able to create favorable impressions.[54] Thus, follow this basic sequence: tell others what you will do, do it, and then showcase what you've done. However, make sure that you actually deliver on your promises. Too many people make lots of noise without actually following through, and this will definitely hurt them down the road.

Finally, depending on your company, you may have to make an effort to work the system yourself prior to year-end discussions. You want to ensure that you are on the radars of key decision makers all year long. Communicate your own view of the year and realistic rating expectations, if possible. This does not have to be too specific (i.e., a specific number isn't required), but if you want to get promoted, people should know why after having met you.

Sure enough, this should be a yearlong exercise. Don't start courting senior colleagues two weeks before the rating sessions. This will reflect negatively on you, as you are clearly trying to win them over at the last minute.

PEOPLE YOU HAVE WORKED WITH

THE PROBLEM

Depending on the size of your company and the industry you are in, you may eventually run the risk of supporting the "wrong" part of the organization. In larger organizations, year-end performance discussions are held within subgroups, meaning that performance discussions do not always include the company's entire leadership. You and your mentor might find limited support for your case simply because of the company's organizational structure.

In one memorable year, I worked on a number of client projects that I fully enjoyed and from which I learned a great deal. However, at year-end, I realized that my peers were in a somewhat better starting position for the final ratings. This was not due to significantly better feedback but rather because I had supported people from another part of the company who had no say in my year-end discussion. My peers had their project managers sitting right in their performance discussions. You can probably guess who had a slight edge.

THE REMEDY

The remedy is simple: If at all possible, try to work for people closer to "home". These do not necessarily have to be with your own team, but the people you will be working for should play at least some role in your final year-end discussion. Obviously, you will have limited say about where to support when you start. You should also maintain a collaborative mindset and lend a helping hand to others in your company if need be. However, keep a somewhat strategic view, and make sure you are not digging your own hole by working for people far from your team for extended periods of time.

LITTLE FEEDBACK

THE PROBLEM

Quality feedback is valuable and having a lot is much better than having little. It is therefore important to have an adequate amount of feedback in any given performance year. Even if this is not common practice in your company, it should be in your own interest to get a regular account of how you have been doing. How else are you going to improve and grow your career?

THE REMEDY

For whatever pieces of work you deliver, ask for feedback. Whether this is internal or external work, mention early that you need feedback and schedule this in your calendar to ensure that it actually gets done. As a rule of thumb, any work performed for more than twenty hours should be considered for feedback. That does not mean you should ask for feedback every twenty hours. However, if you assist on some on-off exercise over some period of time for more than 2.5 full working days, reach out to the person in charge and request some feedback. For specific guidelines on how to receive feedback, see the final section in this chapter.

POOR MENTOR

THE PROBLEM

Depending on how your company conducts performance management, your mentor may be a crucial player in your final performance rating. His or her role starts well before the actual year-end discussion. First of all, your mentor will have to know how to succeed in the company (or industry). For this, you want to have useful and realistic performance objectives. Typically, these are referred to as SMART objectives and should combine personal interests, grade-level performance expectations, and company objectives. Your mentor should be aware of the intricacies of setting and achieving one's objectives and should guide you in defining them up front. In addition, your mentor will have to ensure that you remain on track throughout the year and, as such, hold you accountable.

Finally, if there is a company-wide year-end discussion, you will not be permitted to present your own case. Your mentor will participate on your behalf. If you are unlucky, your mentor will not be properly prepared (e.g., not work the system prior to the session), lack experience (e.g., introducing you first or suggesting unrealistic ratings), show poor engagement (e.g., not actively participating in the discussion), have no internal network to build upon, or even forget the date of your year-end discussion.

THE REMEDY

Pick the right mentor. Apart from being able to work together with your mentor, you need to ensure that he or she can actually provide appropriate support. A good mentor will have several years of experience in the company and a successful track record of past mentor–mentee relationships. To find such a mentor, you might have to ask around. I recommend opting for those who started as juniors in your company themselves, as they will have the best understanding of what works and what does not.

If you are assigned to a mentor who is new to the company, run! Unless he or she is the new star of the industry (unlikely), consider changing your mentor no later than six months into the performance year. For more details on how to change your mentor, see Chapter 12.

These are just some of the potential pitfalls in performance management. Some of these challenges may be more relevant in some organizations than in others. Nonetheless, it helps to be aware of these potential traps and take precautionary action.

How to Receive Feedback

Let's shift our focus to the feedback you receive throughout the year. First, I will provide some general thoughts about feedback, and then I will explain how to best deal with both positive and negative feedback.

The Nature of Feedback

There are many different types of feedback. Again, a lot depends on the nature of the company you are working for. Feedback can be very extensive in written form, via a central reporting system, or just a short conversation at the water cooler. As such, there is no specific guidance on how often you should seek feedback. To be sure, every major work you complete should be supported with specific feedback on your performance. As a rule of thumb, consider anything for which you invested more than twenty hours to require feedback.

Keep in mind though that feedback is very personal. Thus, a lot comes down to individual perception. If you do not click with someone immediately, you may want to seek ways to improve the situation. If you realize only afterward, then learn your lesson. Identify ways to do better next time, or potentially stay away from that person.

What to Do With Negative Feedback

The biggest room in the world is the room for improvement. Try as you might, you will receive feedback on potential development areas. This is just part of life and applies to junior- and senior-level resources alike.

Instead of seeing this as a negative thing, consider all feedback to be constructive. You can always learn something, if only to stay away from a certain person. More specifically, you will want to own the situation either way. Even if you do not agree with the feedback, don't argue with the feedback provider. Instead, show respect, and thank the person for the time taken to provide his or her opinion.

However, when the feedback is a game changer (e.g., something that clearly puts your reputation at risk), immediately get on the phone with or send an email to your mentor. Talk to your mentor about the feedback received, and share your own view. Your mentor will probably also share his or her opinion. Together, agree on how to best deal with the situation. If you do not have a mentor within your firm, consider discussing issues with your manager. Often your mentor will informally reach out to the person that delivered the negative feedback to clarify and ensure that everything is settled before year-end ratings come around.

HOW TO DEAL WITH GOOD FEEDBACK

When you receive positive feedback, don't get too carried away either. Keep working and leverage your newly recognized strengths. For your own development, and to support your mentor, always try to get good feedback in written form. If you received feedback via email or some digital feedback form, this can easily be forwarded to your mentor. No further action would be required.

In case of verbal feedback, you want to go a bit beyond the standard. Follow up with the feedback provider via email, thanking him or her for the discussion and stating the key points mentioned. For example, in Project Insight, Manuela Perez provided Mark with some intermittent feedback to help him in his professional development. Going forward, he should continue leveraging his analytical skills and focus on improving his customer-interviewing skills. He sends the following note the same day:

Dear Manuela,

Thanks for your feedback earlier. I am glad you took the time to provide me with your view, as this will help me in my further development.

Being aware of both my strengths, such as analytical skills, and future development areas, namely customer interviewing (incl. teleconferences), will be very useful.

In case you have nothing to add, I will use this note as additional support for my year-end reference.

Thanks,
Mark

Usually, people do not come back at this point unless you fabricate something completely different from what has been discussed. Unless you hear back within a week, forward this email to your mentor as an FYI. Keep in mind that this note should not replace a more formal written feedback if such a mechanism exists. This is just added on top—a bonus, if you will.

KEY TAKEAWAYS

♦ Recognize the value of performance management. It ensures that effort is duly rewarded by identifying and eliminating poor performers. It also boosts your development by acknowledging your strengths and pointing you toward areas on which to focus.

♦ Deliver outstanding work. At your career start, nothing is as important in determining how quickly you will get ahead as your actual job performance. It's largely a meritocracy for junior-level resources.

♦ Know what to do and when to do it. Understand the performance management cycle and diligently perform your tasks throughout the year. This puts you in a good position for year-end ratings (provided you delivered high-quality work).

♦ Performance ratings lie in the eye of the beholder. As such, the final outcome may not always seem fair. Be aware of the potential pitfalls in having your performance recognized, and take action accordingly.

♦ Request feedback often. Feedback is not only instrumental in your own development but also often forms the basis for your performance rating, so don't leave anything to chance. Actively seek feedback and, ideally, get positive feedback in writing.

PART 3

Not In Your HR Brochure

B Y NOW, WE HAVE discussed how to prepare yourself for your career start and how to get things done on a daily basis. In the following section, I will shed some light on a variety of topics, ranging from managing your private life and preventing yourself from getting screwed by others to effectively pushing back when necessary and finding your sweet spot in the organization.

Irrespective of the company you join, Chapters 15-18 cover topics that are unfortunately rather common. Therefore, it is valuable to give this part a careful read and think about how these concepts might directly apply to you.

[15]

Managing Your Private Life

*"There's no such thing as work–life balance.
There are work–life choices, and you make them,
and they have consequences."*

Jack Welch

AILING TO BALANCE WORK and private life is a recipe for disaster. Work may turn out to be someone's true calling. For the majority, however, there is more to life than just a profession. Unfortunately, we live in times where such a balance often does not exist. Working in certain industries is nothing less than a profound lifestyle decision. Work may get in the way of social activities. In such industries, people have tried to forge a balance before but have found changing the system difficult.

To make matters worse, it is not enough to choose the right industry. I have seen it first-hand in some of my clients that even in supposedly employee-friendly industries, the reality can be much more like a madhouse. At that point, the solution is not to fight but to adapt, and this chapter will show you how.

THE REALITY

If you are lucky, official labor regulations actually matter in your company. However, you would not be an exception if there were no such thing as a nine-to-five workday. You might have to work more. A brief discussion of overtime and taking vacation will make this very clear to you.

ABOUT OVERTIME

Depending on your company, industry, and local regulations, you might have to work overtime. The hours can vary greatly, but do not let the war stories from some people scare you just yet. More often than not, estimates of hours worked are wildly overestimated. I was not safe from this myself and realized that the actual hours worked are lower than you would believe in the heat of the moment.

The reasons for having to work more than planned are many. As said before, you may be juggling both internal and external requests simultaneously. These requests may be more or less urgent, and may be unanticipated. Your company might encourage you to work less. This might even be actively driven by the HR department, but most of the time, juniors will work as long as necessary. And let's not fool ourselves, it initially takes you (junior) longer anyway, but your efficiency will improve with experience. In short, you will work overtime, and you probably won't be compensated for doing so.

VACATION IS KEY

With that in mind, you should obviously take vacations once in a while. Not only are you obligated to take some (if not all) during a given year in most countries, but your employer is probably encouraging you to take time off too. He or she is also obligated, and monetary payouts are not the first choice. The trouble is, there might be a gap between official statements from your company's leadership and actual practice on the ground. Quite simply, work usually takes precedence. If you are involved in some high-profile, time-sensitive piece of work and would like to take vacation, I would not set my hopes too high. The chance of being granted a break can be rather slim, unless:

- There is sudden downtime in the piece of work itself

- Other key personnel are unavailable

- You have received approval to take vacation *before* starting to work on this piece of work[55]

In other words, the only surefire way to take vacation is when you're not involved in some major piece of work. This can be done proactively or reactively. The latter is common for most juniors and basically means that you are taking time off when your task has been accomplished and you are not required to stick around. Clearly, this is not ideal. Your travel plans may have to be rather spontaneous, and you will likely have to travel alone.

Alternatively, you can try to lock in major parts of your annual vacation days in advance. If you have agreed upon and scheduled vacation days, most managers will try to accommodate any future work. How to go about that is what we will look at in the final section of this chapter.

COMMUNICATION WITH YOUR LOVED ONES

It should not come as a surprise that your private life may suffer from your lack of time once you get up and running in your job. Again, it does not have to be like that, but it most certainly can. If you find yourself in such a challenging environment, I recommend you openly address this and tell your loved ones that you will have little time going forward, still want to meet them regularly and therefore have to be a bit more spontaneous (i.e., have to take advantage of any unexpected downtime).

This might not be what many want to hear. I understand that. And it is also not what corporate brochures use to attract high-caliber talent. However, if my interviewees for this book are a realistic sample (which I think they are), then there are workarounds. According to them, open, honest communication is the key to solving a lot of issues (and preventing most to begin with). Let's look at concrete steps that will enable you to make more of your available time.

How to Get the Most out of Your Time

One of the key differences between just starting out and having a more senior role is experience. If you look at your senior colleagues, most of them have learned over the years how to work the system in their favor, including how to maximize their time. There are certain steps that can alleviate the pain. Consider adopting the following four techniques right away.

- **Keep workdays free:** Workdays are for work only. This is not to say that you should forgo any pleasures if you can make time available. You should still take care of yourself. However, try to avoid blocking your evenings with commitments that are not work-related unless you can realistically make it. When things heat up at work, a senior colleague might be able to follow through with his (private) appointment, but you will not. Do not think about fairness here. That does not matter. Instead of always being the one cancelling at the last minute and slowly getting frustrated at yourself, save yourself from this situation to begin with and schedule your private activities, particularly those involving other people, exclusively on weekends.

- **Think of yourself first:** Ensure that you start every day on a high note.[56] That is what successful people do. Do something that is meaningful to you just after waking up. This type of standard morning routine can lay the foundation for a happier and more productive day. Whether it is regular exercise, reading, doing yoga, or learning a language, do not schedule it for "sometime later in the day." That time will never come. It is far too easy to "call it a day" because you're exhausted at 10 p.m.

- **Plan weekends ahead:** In most professions, you will have weekends off and completely to yourself, but that is not always the case. If you find yourself in a more demanding work environment, you need to take action. If you wait until you are absolutely certain that your work is not going to interfere with your weekend, you will most likely not make the most of it. For example, if you wait until Thursday afternoon to make plans for the weekend, chances are that you will not end up doing much—and end up spending your Sunday at the office (or at least sifting through your inbox). I know this because I have been there myself. Even if there was no urgent project work, there was always a plausible reason (i.e., internal work) to go to the office on weekends.

  Be better than that and instead do what the most successful and well-balanced corporate rock stars do. At the beginning of the year, set aside some time with your partner (if applicable) to think about what you would like to do throughout the year. If you want to get away for a weekend trip, decide on a specific weekend. Do this for as many weekends as you can and make preliminary arrangements (e.g., book flights and accommodation). If you do this, you will have a much greater likelihood of actually doing something worthwhile on your weekends. Even if there are busy weeks at the office, you'll figure it out just like prior to taking a vacation when you miraculously end up being the most productive. You will allocate your time accordingly (and if you finish your report while flying to your weekend getaway, then so be it).

- **Plan vacations ahead:** What works for weekends applies to vacation as well. In fact, planning vacations well in advance is probably one of the things I should have learned much earlier myself. Once you have accumulated multiple weeks of vacation days, it will not get any easier to take them. To actually make this happen, you should start early in the year. Set aside some time to go on vacation. Aim to have at least one full two-week vacation during the year (even if this is not common where you work). This will allow you to fully recharge your batteries and go back to work fresh. For specific steps to get your vacation requests approved, see Chapter 16.

Key Takeaways

- Do not be surprised if there is not a solid work–life balance in your industry or company. Work may invariably interfere with private arrangements.

- Be realistic with respect to overtime. In this day and age, working overtime, including on weekends, is not uncommon. However, the majority of "war stories" tend to be exaggerated.

- Take your annual vacation. Up-front planning and early scheduling will increase the likelihood of going on holidays when it suits you, rather than when it suits your manager.

- Ask your family and friends for more spontaneity. Communication is key in garnering their support and understanding.

- Separate work and private life. Block weekdays for work and plan weekends and vacation time in advance.

[16]

Covering Your Ass

"At the end of the day, man, you can't protect yourself from
a haymaker that's coming in toward your face
if you don't see it coming."

Busta Rhymes

S O F A R , W E H A V E covered several topics that form part of the core skill set that every career starter in a large organization should strive to develop. The truth of the matter is that none of this is going to save you every time. There are some situations that require street smarts, but navigating through these unusual situations does not have to be a daunting exercise.

People may try to screw you regardless of what industry you work in. "The likelihood of your daily working life being troubled by a person who is some mixture of psychopaths, Machiavellian and narcissistic is high. If you do not develop the skills to deal with them, they will eat you for breakfast," says psychologist Oliver James[57]. Examples of this could easily fill an entire book. For now, let's clarify why you need to become good at covering yourself and illustrate this point using real-life examples.

WHY YOU NEED TO COVER YOURSELF

Clearly, you should primarily be judged based on the work that you deliver. Unfortunately, that's not the case in the world we live in. When things turn ugly, people often try to cover themselves first.

Early in your career, you are at a significant disadvantage to more experienced colleagues. Unless someone tells you how things work, you will inevitably make mistakes. However, there is no reason to make the same mistake that someone else has made if you can tap into that knowledge and experience.

Communication is everything. As a matter of fact, in most large organizations, you have to take into account that you should be your own marketer. If your personal marketing does not work (i.e., you are largely unknown or have a poor reputation), then you have a problem.

You need to become adept at influencing communication to make your case, particularly when something goes wrong. Your mentor can be your primary guide in this, but it helps to be on top of this yourself. Remember, you are at the bottom of the corporate food chain when you are just starting out. Therefore, the key is to address the root cause of potential issues and learn to take preventive measures.

For illustration purposes, we will use three scenarios that you may experience. These are work screw-ups, managing multiple expectations, and vacations requests. Use these examples as a reference, and try to adapt the underlying concepts to your individual case.

EXAMPLE I: WORK SCREW-UP

Try as hard as you might, sooner or later there will be issues with your work assignments. Sometimes, these are just minor hiccups that can be resolved easily. In rare cases, however, the problems can be more substantial. As a result, you may be reprimanded by your manager for screwing up. If you really were responsible, then there is not much you can do but be humble, apologize, and promise to perform better next time.[58] In such a situation, it is key to really take ownership. Do not put the blame on other people, as this will only make things worse.

However, it may also happen that you had no involvement in the issue caused or even raised your concerns beforehand.[59] At face value, it makes sense to think that this should cover you, but it won't. Your manager (or other senior colleague) has potentially more clout in organizational dynamics, so you should expect him or her to use it if it helps avoid negative consequences for his or her upcoming promotion (not yours!). Your manager has experience and a network that may be leveraged at will in his or her favor. Thus, you could be the first one held accountable for issues you have not caused yourself in order to protect your manager's reputation. Is this the norm? Probably not, but when it happens, there are only two effective ways to mitigate such situations.

- **Have written proof:** You will have to cover yourself before things turn ugly. Therefore, always ensure that you have written proof of what was discussed and what you might have disagreed with. If you can show that your manager actually instructed you to go down a certain route that ultimately led to disaster, that's a good thing.

- **Own the communication:** With your internal mentor, you should agree on one story that both of you will communicate. Obviously, this should be based on truth (at least the way you and your mentor perceive it). Whenever people ask you or your mentor what happened, you can utilize the exact same wording. Consistency and leaving little room for speculation are both essential.

To be sure, none of this is a guarantee that you will not suffer temporarily from a work screw-up. You might, but the above steps will certainly increase the odds of coming out of the situation without long-term consequences.

EXAMPLE II: MANAGING MULTIPLE EXPECTATIONS

In many organizations, you will have a line manager and a team in which everyone has clearly defined roles. However, that is not always the case. You might find yourself supporting multiple stakeholders at the same time. If your company is structured as a matrix organization, potentially juggling two different managers may become the new normal. Either way, you can expect to eventually have to become good at juggling different tasks and responsibilities simultaneously. Remember, as a junior just starting out, you can't just drop certain pieces of work simply because you do not feel like working on them.

Regardless of what these tasks may be, chances are you will run into capacity constraints at some point. I myself learned very quickly that junior-level resources are not in a position to resolve such situations themselves other than by working extra hours. However, what can you do when you might not be able to realistically produce different types of deliverables in time simultaneously? Who should get priority when you have to manage several stakeholders requesting your support and why?

Here is the deal. Do not choose sides. Remain neutral. You do not know the *true* relationship between people, and choosing sides can often backfire. Instead, play the "I'm inexperienced, please show me how" card. Put the ball back into your seniors' courts and let them figure it out. This is one of the few occasions when it is a wise move to sell yourself short.

Taking our case scenario as an example, let's assume that Mark receives a request from Manuela, the Project Lead for Project Insight, to offer support on a presentation. Even though Mark has no availability before the upcoming FT Investor Day, he knows that he cannot simply decline Manuela's request (especially given the importance of the project). Responding directly to the request from Manuela, Mark asks for guidance from Manuela and Jeremiah, the CFO and the one in charge of the Investor Day, using the below format:

Dear Jeremiah and Manuela,

My current capacity is rather stretched. I am therefore kindly asking for your guidance on how to proceed best.

I am currently working toward delivering the documents for the upcoming FT Investor Day by September 16, 2016. Meeting this deadline requires my full attention.

At the same time, I have been asked to provide some support to Project Insight by September 14, 2016.

Right now, I cannot realistically guarantee the timely delivery of both with the quality you would expect.

Please advise on how to serve both of you best. If additional resources can support, I will be happy to provide any assistance necessary.

Thanks a lot for your guidance,
Mark

Mark might still end up working on both requests, which is exactly where he started. However, chances are good that Jeremiah and Manuela can alleviate some of the pressure by finding additional internal resources to support some parts of the work.

EXAMPLE III: VACATION REQUESTS

We all need our breaks, and depending on labor regulations, your employer will be required to ensure that employees enjoy a minimum amount of holidays during any given year. Therefore, in principle, taking a vacation should be straightforward, and most people rarely experience any problems.

The trouble is, there are situations that will require you to change your plans. Unexpected urgent business needs can put previously approved vacation time at risk. Moreover, you would not be the first person whose manager does "not recall" having approved your holidays. To prevent you from having to continuously cancel your holidays on short notice, do what everyone else does with things that matter: get it in writing.

If you are lucky, your company uses a formal vacation request form or software. A standard process makes it infinitely more difficult for others to deny previously approved holidays. In any event, you need to decide on a case-by-case basis how flexible you want to be at that point using the following approach.

REQUESTING VACATION APPROVAL

Ask your manager well in advance when you want to take vacation time. If you do this via email right away, you will want to make your request and then ask for a confirmation. For Mark of Future Technologies this would look as follows:

Dear Jeremiah,

As you are aware, we will work to prepare the quarterly review in the final week of September. As Manuela Perez (CC'd) also will not need my assistance on Project Insight until late October, I consider this a suitable time for me to take some time off.

Unless you planned on me being present, I would like to take this opportunity to go on vacation from October 4–14, 2016.

Please let me know if this would work for you, so I can make the necessary travel arrangements.

Many thanks,
Mark

Note: Mark should schedule a follow-up for one week later, as his vacation request is unlikely to be treated as a top priority.

Confirming Vacation Approval

More often than not, people request vacations in person or over the phone. In these cases, you will have to follow up via email immediately after. This will put you in an infinitely better position when your vacation is being put into question later on. Again, for Finance Analyst Mark this would look as follows:

> *Dear Jeremiah,*
>
> *Thanks a lot for taking the time earlier and approving my planned vacation. As discussed, I will be off from October 4-14, 2016.*
>
> *Many thanks,*
> *Mark*

Key Takeaways

♦ Expect unfair treatment at times. Learn to be street smart when you try to cover yourself, because letting your work speak solely for itself will not always be enough.

♦ Beware of work screw-ups. Managers usually take responsibility, but also understand that you are at a significant disadvantage unless you can back up your case with written correspondence and jointly steer internal communication with your mentor.

♦ Don't try to solve everything. When work requests collide, step back and ask for guidance from those senior people seeking your support. Attempting to prioritize by yourself will likely backfire.

♦ Get vacation requests confirmed in writing. Otherwise, you will always run the risk of having your plans cancelled at short notice.

[17]

Saying No Without Ruining Your Career

"I am only one, but still I am one. I cannot do everything, but still I can do something; and because I cannot do everything, I will not refuse to do something that I can do."

Edward Everett Hale

I F YOU GET THE job done when others won't, you will be popular among your seniors. That is certainly a good thing, but there will be a point when you have to stop taking on further job assignments in order to avoid compromising the quality of your work.

In this chapter, we will look at how to handle such situations. I will share my take on why it's important to push back at times, and most importantly, show you how to do it without ruining your career.

WHY SAYING NO IS IMPORTANT

It is crucial to be selective when you provide support. If you never decline requests coming your way, you will soon experience a work overload that even the best are unable to cope with. Let me be clear:

This is not something you should consider within your first three months. At the start, pushing back should not be your concern.

You will soon notice that some people are more skilled at declining requests than others. Some simply seem to get by without much effort. At each level in the organization, you will meet different people broadly falling into one of four categories: misfits, dreamers, slaves, and drivers. These are distinct groups based on performance and pushback capabilities (Figure 12). Sometimes this is more obvious, and sometimes it is less so. However, once you start paying attention, you can hardly fail to identify those categories in practice.

Misfits joined the company with inaccurate expectations. They are often not very proactive, lack the right skills, or have realized that

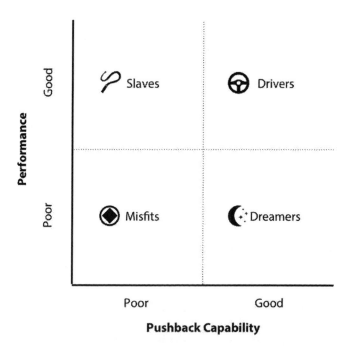

Figure 12: Pushback vs. Performance Categories

the job or industry was not for them. This shows in both their performance and willingness to push back. Their perceived indifference causes them to not last very long.

Dreamers hope to advance their career quickly. This is a good start, but ambition needs to be underpinned by quality work. How often have you met people who thought they were great assets while being average at best? They tend to be strategic in who and what they support (think visibility) using their pushback capabilities. The trouble is, there must be more to the pushback than just noise. Often there is not. Thus, do not try to learn from this group.

Slaves are ambitious and are generally known as nice guys. None of this is bad, but understand that some senior people may exploit this because slaves are easy targets, and they usually get the job done.

Drivers tend to rise quickly in the firm by combining quality work with a reasonable degree of pushback (the main difference between them and "slaves"), and this is the key to a successful career. Drivers know where they are heading, what they are worth, and do not sell out to other people indefinitely, unless they see a way to also gain from it.

Again, focus on delivering great work at first. Over time, sharpen your skills in managing and declining tasks. If you never push back, especially when you are under pressure and there is little to gain from a given task, then you are making a mistake. You have to be somewhat selective, even picky, and develop a reputation for being difficult at times. However, don't come across as difficult just for the sake of it. It helps if you align closely with your manager or someone else you respect. People should know that you are working for _____ (name of person) and think twice before bothering you with their errands.

Should *You* Push Back?

To become a driver in declining requests, consider carefully whether you really want to push back. To help you make this decision, think through the following questions when a request comes your way:

- Do you really have time to work on this request?

- Who is requesting your help? How important is this person in regard to:

  - Your performance rating at year-end

  - Future work opportunities

  - Other internal support (past or future)

- What is the request about? Is it generally in line with your interests or area of expertise?

- Does the request provide any other learning experience or some exposure (to the company or senior leaders)?

Keep these questions in mind. This will become second nature very soon, as you will have a clear idea concerning with whom you want to and should be working. I understand that some organizations may be more rigid, and working collaboratively across different teams may be less common. However, silo thinking is ill-advised in this day and age—particularly if you are about to embark on building a promising career.

There will be requests that you will probably deem unacceptable, but make no mistake, you can shine in each and every situation. For example, organizing catering for a meeting or taking care of late-night printing jobs can be great opportunities to showcase your reliability when you are still relatively unknown in the company. (*Note:* Helping secure your boss's tourist visa for his or her upcoming holiday or picking up your boss' dry cleaning do not fall into this category.) That being said, don't simply decide that certain requests fall below your standard.

How to Push Back

So how do you push back without putting your career prospects on the line? Clearly, there is no one-size-fits-all solution here, but there are certain considerations that you should make when facing such a situation.

To begin with, there is a difference if someone meets you in person to ask for your help rather than contacting you via email. The latter is preferred, as you can carefully consider your options, whereas you might be caught off guard when being approached directly.

However, turning down requests is best when done in person or by phone. Why? Because you don't want this outcome to stick around indefinitely, and you don't want to leave traces. If, for some reason, you cannot push back in person or by phone, do so by writing a carefully crafted email in which you:

- Express gratitude for being considered for the job

- Show interest and motivation to support on that very subject (if applicable)

- State a specific reason for not being able to support this time

- Offer potential solutions (only if these are relevant, and make sure not to suggest fellow colleagues unless they have asked you to)

- Confirm your continued support

When You Do Not Have the Capacity

At times, you might not be able to take on other tasks due to other work priorities. In such a case, you will have to decline the request in order to cover yourself. No one benefits from jobs done poorly or late due to being stretched too thin. Therefore, simply respond by saying:

> *"I would be happy to help, but due to severe capacity constraints, I may not be able to provide the support in the quality you rightly expect."*

The more specific you can be, the better. If you are already supporting some other senior colleague, mention his or her name. This is infinitely more powerful than just saying you had no time.

If all of this does not help, consider escalating the issue. Ideally, this would require a quick chat with whomever you are primarily working for, but at times, even that won't be enough. Let's look at this in sequence.

- **Let the big guys handle it:** Call your manager (or whoever you are working for) to have him or her provide guidance on the issue. State your concerns and ask him or her what the next steps should be. More often than not, you will get a response along the lines of "Leave it to me . . . " in which case your manager will solve the issue for you. If you are given other instructions, get back to the original requestor by email, remembering to Cc your manager and decline once.

  For example, Mark was asked by Manuela to support developing a last-minute presentation for Project Insight. Since he did not have the capacity, Mark agreed with Jeremiah, his boss and head of finance, to turn down the request. He opened his response by writing:

  "As discussed with Jeremiah Smith, . . ."

- **Take matters into your own hands (only when you have to):** If you cannot get in touch with your manager, or if you are in the middle of something urgent that cannot wait while the second requester is pushing you hard, try to resolve the matter on your own. It goes without saying that this is not recommended, but consider it to be an exception. If you still want to go ahead, it is important to be brief and specific in your communication.

Write a short email to both your manager and the requestor that a) asks them to provide guidance on how to proceed best or b) informs them that you cannot satisfy the request at this stage due to the very assignment at hand. A possible script can be found in Chapter 16. Once sent out, get back to your work. Don't engage in follow-up communication until you have accomplished the task you mentioned as your current priority.

To be sure, escalation should not be your default reaction. Keep in mind that some people might be put off by such bold moves. Nevertheless, recognize that there are situations that you will not be able to manage on your own, regardless of what you may think, who you know, or what you have accomplished in the past.

At one point or another, I have made all the mistakes that I am now encouraging you not to make. For example, due to an enormous ramp-up phase in an external client project, some internal work was unlikely to be finished within a given timeframe. In anticipation of this, I reached out to the person in charge of the internal work to explain that I would not be able to continue to support the internal work. I thought this was not only the right thing to do, but I even felt proud of being proactive and raising issues up front. Unfortunately, this did not go over well with the senior person on the other end. What then commenced was what we call "email ping-pong." Known for having a strong hierarchical mindset, this person bombarded me with emails seemingly every minute. Same message, different wording.

Essentially, my concerns were deemed irrelevant, and I was expected to deliver regardless. In the heat of the moment, I simply responded that I had no time to discuss this any further and was sure that our staffing manager would be willing to find someone with available capacity. Don't do this!

The story did not end there. By the following morning, I had received a meeting invitation from that senior person concerning "Ways of Working and Expectations." Mind you, I was well into my second year. I stood my ground, but going forward, this person proved to be a pain when it came to performance ratings and other aspects of my progress.

To put it simply, think twice before trying to solve things on your own. Your actions will most likely backfire. Even so, taking a stand every once in a while will probably not hurt too much.

WHEN YOU ARE JUST NOT INTERESTED

At other times, you might have a lull in your work (you could somehow squeeze this additional task in), but you still don't want to be in charge of a certain task. In such cases, you cannot simply make up additional work as an excuse.

Instead, you have to apply tactics that I learned from a fellow junior colleague on one of my first consulting projects. After having carefully considered the request, you might come to the conclusion that there is simply not much in it for you. Neither the person asking for help nor the request itself brings meaningful benefits. In such cases, take the leap to become a driver and respond by:

- Saying that you are happy to help

- Mentioning any upcoming priorities (to set the right expectation that this might not be an ongoing relationship). For example, in Mark's case, he could reference the upcoming quarterly review and write the following:

"Please note that I will be part of the Finance team preparing the quarterly review beginning September 26, 2016 . . ."

- Requesting feedback upon completion of the job. This is a rule of thumb whenever you work for more than twenty hours on a job.

"To help me in my further development and for upcoming year-end discussions, I would kindly ask you for some short written feedback upon completion of the task."

This is crucial. Few people will be overly enthusiastic about writing yet more feedback, and as a result, the original request will often land on someone else's desk.

KEY TAKEAWAYS

- Learn to turn down requests. Pushing back is a vital skill to enable you to focus on delivering great work when your capacity is already stretched.

- Copy those who have mastered the art of pushback to avoid being exploited. These drivers stand out from misfits, dreamers, and slaves in terms of performance and pushback capabilities.

- Don't be too selective when accepting work requests at the beginning of your career. Regard everything as a learning opportunity, but be mindful if you cannot continue to deliver a superior quality of work.

- Don't overtly push back. Instead, turn to your senior colleagues for guidance and potential mediation.

- Tactically ask for feedback in return for your support when you are not interested in a certain job. Almost magically, those work requests will disappear.

[18]

Stop Thinking and Execute

"It was the Law of the Sea, they said. Civilization ends at the waterline. Beyond that, we all enter the food chain, and not always right at the top."

Hunter S. Thompson,
Generation of Swine: Tales of Shame
and Degradation in the '80s

REGARDLESS OF WHAT INDUSTRY or company you join, before you actually start working, you do not know exactly what you are getting yourself into. Everyone is talking about the great career prospects, the growing business...the list goes on and on. Quite frankly, all that glitters is not gold. Most people will not tell you what it is really like being a junior-level resource in their company and what this actually means for your life.

Make no mistake, perception becomes reality. Whether you agree or not, the way others perceive you directly impacts your standing in the organization and the opportunities you are offered. We have discussed the perception of juniors throughout this book. Chapters 2, 3, 4, and 11 have tackled this subject from different angles.

Now let me offer a more personal take on this process of preparing you for the ultimate cause of frustration, which are the constant requests to do less than you feel capable of doing. At the end of this chapter, you will know exactly what you are getting yourself into and how to best cope with it.

You Don't Know Much

As a junior, you will notice sooner or later that no one cares much about your past accomplishments. Your educational accolades are irrelevant. Where you graduated from might have helped you get the job, but going forward it will matter very little.

By and large, you are supposed to follow instructions and focus on execution. The actual thinking will be taken care of by more experienced colleagues, as you may not be qualified to do so. Whether you like it or not, you will have to earn trust before people start listening to you. You can safely keep your ideas and concerns to yourself for now. You will rarely benefit in any professional way from speaking up this early in the game. Yes, there are exceptions, and if you find that your situation is different, congratulations. Enjoy the ride and take advantage of it.

Obviously, few would ever put it quite like that, but based on my experience, research on the ground, and dozens of interviews with those who have already built successful careers, I am confident that this is the impression many juniors get.

Nobody Said It Was Going to Be Fair

If you're lucky, you're working for someone you can look up to—someone who you fully respect for his or her wisdom, expertise, principles, or experience. That is not going to be the case all the time. In fact, there are more than a few leaders who are far from great.[60] Now, imagine that you are working hard without receiving any recognition for an extended period of time. What will happen? Obviously, it will have a negative impact on your motivation. You will begin to ask yourself why you should keep up the effort and work all those hours, especially when you don't really feel like doing it.

Don't let this deter you. If you buy into the expectation of focusing only on execution, then your creativity will falter. It is as if your brain slowly falls apart due to insufficient exercise. Over time, you stop having ideas, both good and bad. Don't let this happen. Instead, use your mental brain capacity elsewhere.

DON'T LET YOUR MENTAL CAPACITY DETERIORATE

If you have read Chapter 10 on continuous learning, then the following information will sound familiar. I refer to it again because I believe it's crucial. For starters, I encourage you to speak up if you truly feel that you need to. You will likely have to pay a price for doing so, but you will feel better, and, chances are, someone will recognize you and provide invaluable career support. Then again, this will not come without risks. You might end up not lasting very long in the company, but ultimately this is your choice.

If you do not want to risk it and prefer to keep a low profile, at least adopt the two habits already presented in Chapter 10, which are reading every day and writing down new ideas every day. Both habits, if successfully adopted, will ensure that you keep using your idea muscle.

WHEN YOUR BOSS IS REALLY BAD . . .

Finally, let's shed some light on what to do when you're working for a bad manager—or any other senior colleague, for that matter. When I say "bad," I mean "really bad." Personality or character traits aside, we are referring to skills here. So what do you do if you have a manager, or other senior working with you, that you consider completely incompetent? We have all been there at some point. If you have not, trust me, you will have the experience eventually.

Unless you want to leave the company, taking the following principles into account is likely the wisest thing you can do:

- **Continue delivering good work:** No matter how much you suffer, nothing justifies doing a poor job. You have to serve the business first, regardless of whether your manager is competent or not. In fact, if your work helps to advance your manager's career, so be it.

- **Learn from your manager:** Don't waste your time thinking about how bad your manager is, as it will not solve the problem. In fact, he or she probably has some sort of skill set that allowed him or her to be promoted this far. Try to figure out what your manager does well—maybe better than anyone else.[61]

- **Speak to your mentor:** Seek out your mentor for guidance. Chances are, your mentor knows more about your manager's background than you do. Your mentor may also advise you on how to best proceed.

- **Stay close to people you admire:** Identify those colleagues that you really look up to. If they are in your team, working together more closely should be simple. If they are not in your team, get in touch with them anyway, and try to provide them with support if possible. Everyone is happy to receive additional support, and this might be the first step in a long and successful professional relationship. If this is not feasible, at least liaise with them more often over coffee or lunch.

In the bonus material accompanying this book, you can also find a print-friendly infographic about how to deal with a bad boss. Have it within reach for "those" moments. For more information on how to navigate the stakeholder landscape in general, reread Chapters 4 and 11.

ALWAYS LOOK THE PART

Chances are, you will be working in an open-office floor plan. Effects on employee productivity aside (there are lengthy debates about the pros and cons), you should be aware of the ramifications that such layouts can have for you.

Remember, perception is reality. Working in a large open office puts you much more in the spotlight than if you were working in a small office with another colleague or even a cubicle. Many career starters, including some of those interviewed for this book, have repeatedly voiced their concerns about the lack of privacy. Particularly when you are just starting out, it often takes some time to get used to looking the part at all times. Do not mistake a modern office for a workshop. Keep your desk clean and organized. At the bare minimum, tidy up at the end of each workday.

In addition, you have to stay energized, or at least other people should think that you are. Early impressions that you make ultimately shape your reputation within the company. Don't take any risks here if you can. Instead, try to maintain an adequate energy level throughout the day. If you have too laid back of an attitude, your name might easily end up on some list of dismissals (I've seen this first-hand).

TAKE THINGS MORE LIGHTLY

You should perceive your work as important. Ultimately, it will at least have a direct impact on your own career progression. Nevertheless, be somewhat realistic. Do not overestimate your importance in other people's minds, particularly more senior colleagues. Do not take it personally when you have to follow up and remind them about certain things numerous times. Most likely, they are simply drowning in work themselves, and, while your work may be important, there are other items of much higher priority. So take it lightly.

KEY TAKEAWAYS

- Forget previous accolades and accomplishments. They are largely irrelevant. Expect many senior colleagues to ask juniors to focus on executing what they have "dreamed" up.

- Never get discouraged. Work on yourself and keep your mind active through regular reading and seeking to become an idea machine.

- Learn from each experience. Over time, carve out your sweet spot in the organization by identifying and staying close to people whose values you share. Remember that you cannot change the system.

- Always look professional. Stay energized and organized throughout the day, because, after all, perception is reality.

- Understand that you are probably not as important as you think. Do not expect to be a top priority for most of your colleagues, including your boss. Everyone has his or her own agenda.

PART 4

Fresh Start

LIFELONG EMPLOYMENT IS DEAD. Tenures get shorter. Multiple careers in a lifetime are the new normal. As such, a junior's life cycle would not be complete if it did not include a potential end of the career stage that you have just started. This is what we will focus on in the subsequent pages. Chapter 19 provides a decision-making framework for when you first start thinking about jumping ship. Chapter 20 explicitly lays out what should be done—and why—in case one decides to leave.

[19]

When You Might Want to Quit

"Would you tell me, please, which way I ought to go from here?"
"That depends a good deal on where you want to get to," said the Cat.
"I don't much care where—" said Alice.
"Then it doesn't matter which way you go," said the Cat.

Lewis Carroll,
Alice's Adventures in Wonderland

EVEN THE BEST WORK environment can turn sour, and you might start thinking about whether to move on. You will ask yourself if this company or industry is really for you. You will start questioning whether you would benefit from starting fresh elsewhere. You will ponder whether to seek out new opportunities by perhaps joining a competitor or even a start-up. This chapter will not give you the answers to these questions, but it will provide you with a structured decision-making framework once your initial questioning has become more material.

GOING BACK TO WHERE IT ALL STARTED

Before spending too much time thinking about whether to change careers or not, you should look at your current situation from a different angle. Instead of weighing the pros and cons of making a change, first consider where you have come from. Think about what originally got you into this current position. If you have done the personal pitch in Chapter 2, then review your answers to Questions 6 and 7 about your expectations.

The decision tree (Figure 13) will guide you in determining whether or not a change is truly necessary, and, if so, what that change may be. It is crucially important to work through this exercise with full honesty. Otherwise, the exercise is essentially pointless.

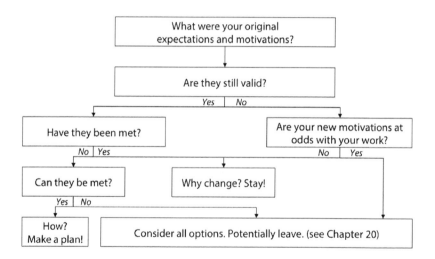

Figure 13: Career Change Decision Tree

THINKING IT THROUGH

If you have found that your current work is not in line with your core motivation or original expectations, you should consider alternative options. To do this systematically, answer the following questions:

1. What is your ultimate objective? Think about what you want to accomplish. Clarify what success means to you. Most likely, you will come up with a handful of different aspects that are important to you. Since they are hardly equal in importance, go ahead and prioritize them.

2. What are your options? List all the options you have when leaving your job. Be realistic, but don't limit your imagination too much. Transferring to another department or internationally?[62] Joining a competitor in the same industry? Changing industries? Starting your own business? Traveling the world? Doing a PhD? There are countless options. It is completely up to you.

3. What is there to gain from each option? Be specific about the potential benefits from each option.

4. What are the downsides of each option? Most decisions require a trade-off. By opting for one, you will likely have to forgo something else. What aspect of each of your options do you consider less than ideal? In other words, what don't you like about the probable impact from choosing any one option?

5. Which options can you eliminate right away? Based on your assessment of both pros and cons, which options appear to be completely at odds with your ideal outcome? Reduce the number of options down to two or three at most.

6. How could you mitigate remaining downsides? When considering your final option(s), try to identify ways to mitigate the negative aspects. This will help you identify the best option and should help to include all of your desired objectives from Step 1.

7. What is the next step? Whatever your final decision, ensure that you follow through. Use the momentum gained from this exercise and decide on the next several steps, if possible. Do at least one thing today, and schedule the rest for the future. This increases the likelihood of actually moving closer to your goal.

Do not feel obliged to stay put. "You must see your career [...] as a journey with twists and turns rather than a straight line," says strategy expert Greene.[63] Considering all this, what is your ultimate decision? It's crucial to spend some time on this choice and not rush ahead.

KEY TAKEAWAYS

♦ Be open to new ventures. Career changes are common in all industries. Your industry is likely no different.

♦ Make career decisions systematically. Use a structured decision-making process to determine whether a career change is indeed necessary. Oftentimes, minor steps can be taken to avoid the process of changing firms or industries.

♦ Identify and evaluate all viable career change options. This process lays the groundwork for a more satisfying career track if your current position is no longer meeting your objectives.

[20]

If You Decide to Quit

*"The hardest thing to learn in life is
which bridge to cross and which to burn."*

David Russell

THIS IS THE FINAL chapter, and in a way, this will close the loop. This chapter assumes that you have decided to leave your current position, as discussed in Chapter 19. Against that background, we will now look at *how* you should leave.

Contrary to what many may say, burning bridges is the wrong thing to do. Leaving a work environment requires ticking boxes in two categories: professional and personal. The professional category is all about your previously established work commitments and areas of responsibility. This is what we will discuss first. We will look at what you need to do in order to avoid having things fall apart once you are gone.

We will then focus on the personal category, which is about the relationships you have developed in your company. We will discuss how to set up your relationships for the future within the process of saying goodbye.

LAYING THE GROUNDWORK FOR YOUR DEPARTURE

Once you have decided to leave the firm, you will have to finalize your departure. The exact process may differ between companies, but by and large, to accomplish this you will want to arrange your departure with your boss and HR and clear the way for departure. Let us look at both steps in more detail.

ARRANGING YOUR DEPARTURE WITH YOUR BOSS AND HR

Making the decision to leave is not an easy one. Telling your boss, who has hired you, is even trickier. Even if your boss is one of the reasons for your resignation, you will likely feel uncomfortable bringing up the topic of leaving (particularly if this is the first time you are doing this). Nevertheless, don't spend too much time waiting (and second-guessing) before you seek a final discussion with your boss. Find time in his or her agenda and prepare as you would for any other important conversation (e.g., a job interview). When you meet your boss, be absolutely clear about what you want. Your decision should already be made. Now, it's just about agreeing on details, such as leaving dates, holiday payout, etc.

In addition, you should clearly understand and be able to explain the reasons why you're leaving and the exact wording thereof. Of course, you could tell your boss that he or she "sucks," but you can probably predict what that would mean for your reputation within the company as well as any future relationships with your colleagues. You will want to be authentic but also tactful. Therefore, inform your boss about your departure and:

- State that your decision is final

- Make it clear that this decision was not an easy one to make and you've thought it through

- Thank him or her for the trust and learning opportunities you have received from the company

- Emphasize that this is not a decision against the company or its people, but solely for personal reasons

- Mention a reason for your choice (e.g., change of environment, the industry or type of work is not for you, family, etc.)

- Confirm that all of your tasks and responsibilities will either be completed or officially handed over to others prior to your departure

- Ask to stay in contact with him or her even after you have left

You would not be the first employee to become completely disillusioned once you announce your exit to your boss. Chances are, you will be asked to keep a low profile and not tell other people about your move. Acknowledge your boss's concerns by stating that you respect his or her views and will work toward minimizing any disruptions as much as possible. This means that you will not engage in any badmouthing; instead, you will use the time available to nurture existing relationships.

You should also not be surprised when the relationship between you and your boss, as well as other members of the team, changes drastically from one day to the next. Some people tend to take it personally when a member of the team decides to go a different way. They feel mistreated and all trust is often lost. You can't do much about this. You need to understand that this might happen, but continue to maintain your professional attitude and follow your own path.

Apart from meeting your boss, you will have to align on administrative requirements with your HR department. They will usually provide you with a checklist of things to complete prior to leaving. This should be rather straightforward. Most likely, the talk with HR will be a breeze. They are used to having these discussions and will therefore not make it more difficult on you than necessary. Chances are, they will ask for what triggered your decision to leave or inquire about things the company could improve. Remain professional. Whatever list of items you have on your mind that you would have wished someone had improved in your company, I recommend you keep this to yourself. It is great to help others improve, but you do not know how this feedback will be translated and channeled back into the organization. Do not put your long-term reputation at risk. State your reasons for leaving (ideally, the same reasons you provided to your boss), and move on.

Clearing Your Way to Departure

One of the things you should have mentioned to your boss is how to deal with ongoing tasks and responsibilities. You cannot simply drop everything once you have agreed to leave the company. Most likely, your boss will have his or her own expectations of what needs to be finalized before your departure. Whether you are given a list of items to cross off or not, you should spend some of your own time identifying all the items that you are currently associated with in some form or other. To accomplish this, think through the following questions:

- What tasks are you currently working on, either by yourself or as part of a team? What other tasks have you been assigned to? What roles do you perform?

- What is the state of each of those tasks or roles?

- What are the next steps for each of those tasks or roles?

- Which of the upcoming steps can be accomplished personally, and by when can you complete them?

- If any other next steps need to be completed or continued by someone else, who will have the capacity and willingness to do so? Thus, whom can you hand these tasks over to?

Once you have worked through the above questions, come up with a concise plan of how to finalize all this. The objective of this exercise is to cover yourself by preventing things from falling apart when you leave. You can (and should) proactively communicate this plan to your boss before your departure. This will give him or her further confidence in your professionalism and will minimize any potential negative sentiments toward you once you are gone.

YOU ALWAYS MEET TWICE

Apart from terminating all your work commitments, let's look at the personal aspect of farewell management. You will want to make sure that the connections you have invested in over months or years are not lost once you leave the company. There is a German idiom that literally translates to, "You always meet people twice in a lifetime." While the original meaning is more about doing unto others as you would have them do unto you, I believe in the idea of repeat encounters in a completely different context. With that in mind, it is crucial not only to build but also to maintain your network when you make the choice to move on.

To accomplish this, do what works in any networking context. Come up with a plan and focus on execution. I will show you what this translates to in most industries and how to do this in the remainder of this chapter.

5-STEP PROCESS TO LEAVING THE FIRM AND TAKING RELATIONSHIPS WITH YOU

In order to maintain your relationships, you will have to proceed strategically. This is best accomplished by following a tried-and-tested 5-step process.

1. List key people: Come up with a list of all those people that you deem important. These might be colleagues with whom you are friends, colleagues you have learned something from, or simply people you like or sincerely respect. This list may be a long one. Don't limit your list to your peers, either; consider junior and senior colleagues alike.

2. Meet key people individually: Go through the list and identify key people you would like to meet with individually. Depending on agendas, you should agree to meet for coffee, lunch, dinner, or in any other non-work environment to have some personal conversation. These occasions will serve as crucial moments to connect. You will be able to:

    – Express your gratitude for their support (or whatever applies)

    – Clarify your reasoning for leaving the company directly to them

    – Speak about potential next steps

3. Invite all people: Invite all of the people you listed in Step 1 to a final round of farewell drinks. The invitation should be sent out as one message at least two weeks in advance. Whether the drinks are scheduled before or after your actual leaving date does not really matter. If you

can afford it, pay for the drinks and snacks. Regard this occasion as an investment in your future.

4. Make yourself findable online: This is a no-brainer. Unless you have been living under a rock, you should have various social media profiles by this time. If not, now is the time to set them up. Focus primarily on professional networks, such as LinkedIn or Xing.

5. Stay connected: Sift through the list of people, and see if you are connected with them online. Ideally, you will want to have all of them as contacts in your professional network.

How About the Leaving Email?

Many people think about taking their network of relationships beyond their current employer. However, they only do this halfheartedly and usually at the last minute. Let's be clear. It is not enough to send a farewell email to "Corporate All" on the day of your departure. It is also useless to request ongoing contact by providing private contact details. Ninety-nine percent of the time, this email will not be followed up upon in any way.

You have to take matters into your own hands and connect proactively. Make the first step. Don't wait for others to connect with you.

Key Takeaways

♦   Don't burn bridges. Nurture key relationships and take them beyond your current employer when leaving the company. Lay the foundation for ongoing relationships.

♦   Inform your boss about your intended departure first. Reiterate that your resignation will cause minimal disruptions to the business because you will finalize open items or conduct thorough handovers.

♦ Invest in your departure. Individual catch-ups (e.g., over lunch or coffee) and a common farewell event can serve as practical investments to leave on a positive note.

Final Thoughts

These are things that have worked for me and others. Will they work for you? Maybe. I don't know, but I hope so. At the very least, I am convinced that *Got the Job... Now What?* will put you on the right track, provided that you actually use the guidance in here.

What we have covered in this book are the primary dos and don'ts when starting a corporate career. Surviving the first two to three years is crucial, as it lays the foundation for many years to come. However, it is also just the beginning of a much longer journey. Therefore, ambition and determination aside, have patience. Sometimes, things simply take a little longer to play out.

In *Success and Luck*, Robert Frank identifies the three building blocks of success based on his research: talent, effort, and luck.[64] Without talent, you have a rather unfortunate starting position. If you have secured a job, you must be equipped with talent in one form or another. At least someone else must believe that is the case. Do not let that person down.

Then there is effort. As I have stressed in this book, delivering great work and going the extra mile are essential. By picking up this book and actually reading it, I am confident that you are well aware of that fact. Effort is vital. Never lose that mindset.

That being said, talent and effort are not enough. You also need to have luck. This is what many of those interviewed for this book have reportedly had. Whether it was landing the job in the first place, making a brave move, or having a great manager to learn from, not all things have been under their direct control. This might be true for many others, including you.

The nature of luck is that you cannot force it, but when it strikes, you must be ready to take advantage. That readiness is what you can and should work on by developing your craft. Ultimately, everything that matters is a skill—and skills can be learned. If one person can learn it, anyone can learn it, and so can you. For some, it might be easier than for others; we call those people talented. However, as long as you realize that skills can be learned, nothing stands in your way in the long term. Whatever you are going to focus on learning next, *Got the Job... Now What?* has countless lessons that can help you do so.

Now, it is up to you to apply the concepts from this book. Make sure you truly own them. Make them yours. Don't blindly copy me (or anyone, for that matter). Stay authentic, and use your own style because that—your personality—is what ultimately makes you stand out.

Appendix

In this part, I have included some additional resources that you might find useful. Primarily, they include books that have either influenced me or my colleagues, or those we consider to be must-reads in the given field.

PRESENTATION DESIGN

- Reynolds, Garr. Presentation Zen: Simple Ideas on Presentation Design and Delivery. Berkeley, CA: New Riders Pub., 2008.

- Duarte, Nancy. Slide:ology: The Art and Science of Creating Great Presentations. Beijing: O'Reilly Media, 2008.

NETWORKING AND RELATIONSHIP BUILDING

- Ferrazzi, Keith, and Tahl Raz. Never Eat Alone: And Other Secrets to Success, One Relationship at a Time. New York: Random House, 2005.

- Carnegie, Dale. How to Win Friends and Influence People. New York: Pocket Books, 1998.

CAREER BUILDING

- Newport, Cal. So Good They Can't Ignore You: Why Skills Trump Passion in the Quest for Work You Love. New York: Business Plus, 2012.

- Arden, Paul. It's Not How Good You Are, It's How Good You Want to Be. London: Phaidon, 2003.

- Peters, Thomas J. The Brand You 50, or, Fifty Ways to Transform Yourself from an "Employee" into a Brand That Shouts Distinction, Commitment, and Passion! New York: Knopf, 1999.

COMMUNICATION, WRITING, AND STRUCTURED THINKING

- Heath, Chip, and Dan Heath. *Made to Stick: Why Some Ideas Survive and Others Die.* New York: Random House, 2007.

- Hertz, Noreena. *Eyes Wide Open: How to Make Smart Decisions in a Confusing World.* London: William Collins, 2013.

- Minto, Barbara. *The Pyramid Principle: Logic in Writing and Thinking.* London: Financial Times Prentice Hall, 2002.

EXCEL MASTERY

- Bendoly, Elliot. Excel Basics to Blackbelt: An Accelerated Guide to Decision Support Designs. Cambridge: Cambridge UP, 2008.

- Jelen, Bill, and Michael Alexander. Excel 2013 Pivot Table Data Crunching. New York: Pearson Education, 2013.

Time Management

- Glei, Jocelyn K. Manage Your Day-to-Day: Build Your Routine, Find Your Focus, and Sharpen Your Creative Mind. Las Vegas: Amazon Publishing, 2013.

- Belsky, Scott. Making Ideas Happen: Overcoming the Obstacles between Vision and Reality. New York: Portfolio, 2010.

- Covey, Stephen. The 7 Habits of Highly Effective People: Powerful Lessons in Personal Change. New York: Free Press, 2004.

Reading Effectively

- Tim Ferriss' blog post "Scientific Speed Reading: How to Read 300% Faster in 20 Minutes", here: http://fourhourworkweek. com/2009/07/30/speed-reading-and-accelerated-learning/

- Chapter 7 in Pozen, Richard C. *Extreme productivity: Boost your results, reduce your hours.* New York: HarperBusiness, 2012.

- Kump, Peter. *Breakthrough Rapid Reading.* New York: Prentice Hall Press, 1999.

Bibliography

Altucher, Claudia Azula & James Altucher (2014). *Become an Idea Machine: Because Ideas Are the Currency of the 21st Century*. CreateSpace Independent Publishing.

Association for Talent Development (2015). *2015 State of the Industry*. Alexandria, Virginia.

Barney, Jay & Trish G. Clifford (2010). *What I Didn't Learn in Business School: How strategy works in the real world*. Boston: Harvard Business Review Press.

Carnegie, Dale (2007). *How to Win Friends and Influence People*. London: Vermillion.

Chui, Michael (2013). *The Social Economy Unlocking Value and Productivity through Social Technologies*. New York: McKinsey & Company.

Cialdini, Robert B. (2007). *Influence: The Psychology of Persuasion*. New York: Collins.

Citrin, James M. (2015). *The Career Playbook: Essential Advice for Today's Aspiring Young Professional*. New York: Crown Business.

Covey, Stephen (2004). *The 7 Habits of Highly Effective People: Powerful Lessons in Personal Change*. New York: Free Press.

Danziger, Shai, Jonathan Levav, and Liora Avnaim-Pesso. "Extraneous Factors in Judicial Decisions." *Proceedings of the National Academy of Sciences*, 2011, 6889–92.

Ellsberg, Michael (2011). *The Education of Millionaires: It's not what you think and it's not too late*. New York: Penguin.

Ericsson, Karl Anders (1996). *The Road to Excellence: The Acquisition of Expert Performance in the Arts and Sciences, Sports, and Games*. Mahwah, N. J.: Lawrence Erlbaum Associates.

Ferriss, Timothy (2007). *The 4-Hour Workweek: Escape 9–5, Live Anywhere, and Join the New Rich.* New York: Crown Publishers.

Frank, Robert (2016). *Success and Luck: Good Fortune and the Myth of Meritocracy.* Princeton: Princeton University Press.

Gamber, Olivia (2015). *The Career Upgrade Roadmap: 90 Days to a Better Job and a Better Life.* CreateSpace Independent Publishing.

Glei, Jocelyn K., and Scott Belsky (2013). *Maximize your potential: Grow your expertise, take bold risks and build an incredible career.* Las Vegas: Amazon Publishing.

Godin, Seth (2012). *The Icarus Deception: How High Will You Fly?* New York: Penguin.

Goleman, Daniel, and Richard E. Boyatzis. *Primal Leadership: Unleashing the Power of Emotional Intelligence.* Tenth Anniversary ed., Boston: Harvard Business Review Press, 2013.

Greene, Robert (2012). *Mastery.* New York: Viking.

Hartley, Simon (2012). *How to Shine: Insights into unlocking your potential from proven winners.* Chichester, UK: Capstone Publishing.

Hoffer, Eric (2006). *Reflections on the human condition.* Titusville, NJ: Hopewell Publications.

Hunt-Davis, Ben & Harriet Beveridge (2011). *Will It Make the Boat Go Faster?: Olympic-winning strategies for everyday success.* Leicester: Matador.

James, Oliver (2013). *Office politics: how to thrive in a world of lying, backstabbing and dirty tricks.* London: Vermilion.

Janssen, Christian P., Gould, S. J., Li, S. Y., Brumby, D. P. & A. L. Cox (2015). Integrating knowledge of multitasking and interruptions across different perspectives and research methods. *International Journal of Human-Computer Studies, 79,* 1-5.

Jensen, Bill, and Josh Klein (2010). *Hacking Work: Breaking Stupid Rules for Smart Results.* London: Penguin Books.

Johnson, Steven (2010). *Where Good Ideas Come From: The Natural History of Innovation.* New York: Riverhead Books.

Kelly, Kevin (2016). *The Inevitable: Understanding the 12 Technological Forces That Will Shape Our Future.* New York: Viking.

Kerr, Hillary & Katherine Power (2016). *The Career Code: Must-Know Rules for a Strategic, Stylish, and Self-Made Career.* New York: Harry N. Abrams.

Kotter, John Paul, & Holger Rathgeber (2006). *Our iceberg is melting: Changing and succeeding under any conditions.* New York: St. Martin's Press.

Lowndes, Leil (2003). *How to talk to anyone: 92 little tricks for big success in relationships.* Chicago, IL: Contemporary Books.

Metros, Susan E. (2006). The Importance of Mentors. In C. Golden (Ed.), Cultivating Careers: Professional development for campus IT (pp. 5.1-5.13). Educause.

Ophir, Eyal, Nass, Clifford & Anthony D. Wagner (2009). Cognitive control in media multitaskers. *Proceedings of the National Academy of Sciences,* 106(37), 15583-15587.

Pfeffer, Jeffrey (2010). *Power: Why Some People Have It—and Others Don't.* New York: Harper Business.

Pozen, Richard C. (2012). *Extreme productivity: Boost your results, reduce your hours.* New York: HarperBusiness.

The Radicati Group (2015). *Email Statistics Report 2011–2015.* Palo Alto, CA.

Ramo, Joshua (2016). *The Seventh Sense: Power, Fortune, and Survival in the Age of Networks.* New York: Little, Brown and Company.

Ressler, Cali & Jody Thompson (2008). *Why work sucks and how to fix it: The results-only revolution.* New York: Portfolio.

Roth, Alvin E. (2015). *Who Gets What and Why:* The New Economics of Matchmaking and Market Design. New York: Mariner Books.

Runde, James A. (2016). *UNEQUALED: Tips for Building a Successful Career Through Emotional Intelligence.* Hoboken, New Jersey: John Wiley & Sons.

Vanderkam, Laura (2012). *What the Most Successful People Do Before Breakfast: A Short Guide to Making Over Your Mornings--and Life.* New York: Penguin.

Wolff, Hans-Georg & Klaus Moser (2009). Effects of networking on career success: A longitudinal study. *Journal of Applied Psychology,* 94, 196-206.

Notes

1   Godin, Seth. "Do You Have the Right to Be Heard?" http://sethgodin.ty-pepad.com/seths_blog/. June 26, 2010. Accessed May 24, 2015.

2   www.businessinsider.com/how-google-hires-people-2013-6?IR=T

3   www.gsb.stanford.edu/insights/diverse-backgrounds-personali-ties-can-strengthen-groups

4   www.forbes.com/sites/jeannemeister/2012/08/14/job-hopping-is-the-new-normal-for-millennials-three-ways-to-prevent-a-human-re-source-nightmare/#4dccb84e5508

5   See Hartley, S. (2012)

6   See Lowndes, L. (2003)

7   See Greene, R. (2012)

8   See Carnegie, D. (2007)

9   This applies to all corporate divisions and functions. A common mis-conception is to think in silos only, and forget to see the big picture. Ultimately, it does not matter whether you are in sales, HR, or finance. You are all sitting in the same boat, and the destination is success in the marketplace.

10 See Citrin, J. M. (2015)

11 See Hartley, S. (2012)

12 See Hartley, S. (2012)

13 See Barney, J. B. & Clifford, T. G. (2010)

14 If you are willing to pay the price, and reap the benefits, then make this your *modus operandi*.

15 See Citrin, J. M. (2015)

16 See The Radicati Group (2015)

17 See Chui, M. (2013)

18 This is independent of company size. There are Fortune 500 firms where any attachment larger than 10 MB will be blocked.

19 Whenever you use USB keys for work purposes, make sure they are encrypted.

20 See Gamber, O. (2015)

21 See Ressler, C. & Thompson, J. (2008)

22 See Danziger et al. (2011)

23 See Ophir et al. (2009)

24 See Janssen et al. (2015)

25 See Covey, S. (2004)

26 See Pozen, R. C. (2012)

27 www.wunderlist.com

28 See Pozen, R. C. (2012)

29 See Ellsberg, M. (2011)

30 See Kotter, J. P. & Rathgeber, H. (2006)

31 See Ramo, J. (2016)

32 See Hoffer, E. (2006)

33 See Ellsberg, M. (2011)

34 See Greene, R. (2012)

35 See Glei, J. K. & Belsky, S. (2013)

36 See Hunt-Davis, B. & Beveridge, H. (2011)

37 See Ericsson, K. A. (1996)

38 See Ferriss, T. (2007)

39 See Johnson, S. (2010)

40 Altucher, James. "The Ultimate Guide for Becoming an Idea Machine." Altucher Confidential. 2014. Accessed May 24, 2015.

41 See Altucher, C. A. & Altucher, J. (2014)

42 See Lowndes, L. (2003)

43 See Wolff, H.-G. & Moser, K. (2009)

44 See Ellsberg, M. (2011)

45 See Runde, J. A. (2016)

46 See Greene, R. (2012)

47 See Greene, R. (2012)

48 See Metros, S. E. (2006)

49 See Glei, J. K. & Belsky, S. (2013)

50 See Hartley, S. (2012)

51 See Barney, J. B. & Clifford, T. G. (2010)

52 See Association for Talent Development (2015)

53 SMART is an abbreviation for objectives or goals that are *Specific*, *Measurable*, *Achievable*, *Relevant*, and *Time-Bound*.

54 See Pfeffer, J. (2010)

55 Sure enough, this is no guarantee you will actually end up taking your holidays. There will be situations in which you may be asked to cancel your arrangements.

56 See Vanderkam, L. (2012)

57 See James, O. (2013)

58 See Kerr, H. & Power, K. (2016)

59 If you are working on some extraordinary project, it is recommended that you never start without setting up a risk and issue tracker. Take the initiative in case your manager does not request this.

60 See Goleman, D. & Boyatzis, R. E. (2013)

61 See Greene, R. (2012)

62 Career tracks do not have to follow a straight line. Zigzagging within corporations or industries can get you ahead, too.

63 See Greene, R. (2012)

64 See Frank, R. (2016)

Made in the USA
Charleston, SC
18 December 2016